CHALLENGING LEVEL

# The Odyssey

## A Teaching Guide

by Mary Elizabeth

Illustrations by Kathy Kifer

Journey Strand

**Dedicated to
my son, Michael**

*The Odyssey*
Translated by W. H. D. Rouse
Mentor Books
New American Library, Inc.
Copyright © 1937 New American Library, Inc.  All rights reserved.
PO Box 999
Bergenfield, NJ 07621

*The Odyssey*
Translated with an introduction by
Richmond Lattimore
Harper Torchbooks
Harper & Row, Publishers
Copyright © 1965, 1967 HarperCollins.  All rights reserved.
10 East 53rd St.
New York, NY 10022

*The Odyssey*
Translated by Robert Fitzgerald
Passages printed by permission of Random House, Inc.
Vintage Books
A Division of Random House, Inc.
Copyright © 1990 Random House, Inc.  All rights reserved.
Mail Drop 28-2, 201 E. 50th St.
New York, NY 10022

*The Odyssey*
Translated by Robert Fagles
Introduction and Notes by Bernard Knox
Viking Penguin
Penguin Books USA Inc.
Copyright © 1996 Penguin USA.  All rights reserved.
375 Hudson Street
New York, NY 10014

*The Odyssey: A Stage Version*
Derek Walcott
Copyright © 1993 Derek Walcott
Reprinted by permission of Farrar, Straus & Giroux, Inc.
Farrar, Straus & Giroux, Inc.
19 Union Square West
New York, NY 10003

Copyright © 1999  Garlic Press

Teaching Guide Published by:
**Garlic Press**
605 Powers St.
Eugene, OR  97402

ISBN 0-931993-92-X
Order Number GP-092

# TABLE OF CONTENTS

# TABLE OF CONTENTS

# NOTES TO THE TEACHER

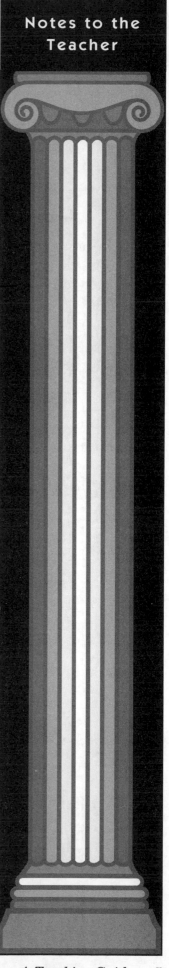

The Discovering Literature Series is designed to develop a student's appreciation for good literature and to improve reading comprehension. At the Challenging Level, we focus on a variety of reading strategies that can help students construct meaning from their experiences with literature as well as make connections between their reading and the rest of their lives. The strategies reflect the demands of each literature selection. In this study guide, we will focus on epic, translations, background, mythology, beginning a book, plot, setting, the heroic journey, and characterization. The following discussion explains the various elements that structure the series at the Challenging Level.

## THE ORGANIZATION OF THIS LITERATURE GUIDE

Each book analysis is organized into two basic elements: **Journal and Discussion Topics** and **Book Summary.** One or more of the Journal and Discussion Topics can either be displayed on the board or on an overhead projector before each book is read. The selected Journal and Discussion Topics will help to focus the students' reading of the book. Choose questions that will not give away important plot elements. Because there are so many translations used in classrooms, this Literature Guide does not feature lists of **Book Vocabulary.** It is, however, appropriate during prereading activities to introduce vocabulary words that you think students will need in order to insure that their reading is not disrupted by the frequent need to look up a word. Guide students in using one of the vocabulary exercises from page 6.

• The **Journal and Discussion Topics** include directions for the students' **Reader Response Journals** and questions for **Discussion.** These topics will help the students become engaged with the literature. Students will benefit by reading with their journals beside them so they can easily note any unfamiliar vocabulary that was not presented to the class, questions they have about the literature, and their own reactions as they enter into the experience of the story. Journals can also be used for written dialogue between you and students. If you wish, periodically collect the journals and respond to students' comments. It is important for students to know beforehand whether their journals are private or public. In either case, journals should not be corrected or graded but only recorded as being used. You may also wish to keep your own journal.

• **Discussion** can take place between partners, in small groups, or in a whole-class setting. Students may also wish to reflect on the discussion in their journals. Discussion starters include

1. A group retelling of the book in which everyone participates.
2. Each group member telling the most striking moment in the book for him or her.
3. Each group member telling a question she or he would like to ask the author or a character about the book.
4. Each student telling what he or she liked most or least about the book.
5. A discussion of how the book relates to the preceding book and the rest of the text that has already been read.

Discussion can end with predictions for what will happen in the next book. Each student should note predictions in her or his journal.

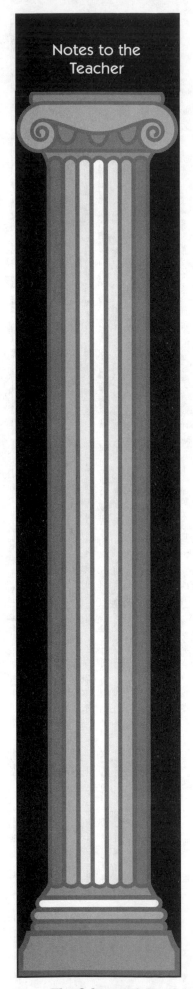

Always ask students to retell (or summarize) the material. The retelling can be oral, artistic (for example, a storyboard), or prose. Retelling can take place in the discussion groups or in the journals.

• Suggestions for teaching **Vocabulary** include

1. Finding relationships between and among words helps students learn the words better than treating them separately. Have students create a web or other graphic showing the relationships between and among the vocabulary words. Encourage them to add other related words to their web.
2. A group of words that is primarily nouns can be used to label a picture.
3. Have students use the words in a piece of writing, for example, a poem, a 1-act play, a diary entry written from the point of view of one of the characters.
4. Have students research the etymology of each word and keep notes.
5. Have students make and exchange crossword puzzles based on the vocabulary words.
6. Have students write and exchange a cloze exercise using the vocabulary words. A cloze exercise has a blank for each vocabulary word, and the surrounding context must clearly indicate which word belongs in each blank.

• The **Book Summary** for each book is included for teacher use. It provides an at-a-glance scan of the book events. Use it to refresh your memory about the contents of each book.

### The Groupings of Literature

We have among our titles a group of works that could be presented as part of a unit called "The Journey." We present groupings of literature so that you can easily present works as a unit. The works of literature resonate with each other, providing a multi-faceted look at a variety of **themes** such as

- The journey as a metaphor
- Coping with change
- Safety versus risk-taking
- Change is opportunity (a Chinese saying)
- Choices
- Trust
- Flexibility
- The journey versus the arrival
- Resourcefulness

Since no substantial work of literature has only a single theme, "The Journey" is not the only possible grouping for the works of literature. But references to themes can both help focus students' attention as they read and help them link works of literature together in meaningful ways. In a similar way, a grouping of books can throw light on **Big Ideas**. Big Ideas worth considering include the following:

- How does context (cultural, social, etc.) affect us?
- How should personal desire be balanced with other responsibilities?
- What circumstances lead to personal development and growth?
- How is place important in our lives? What kinds of changes can occur when we change our location?

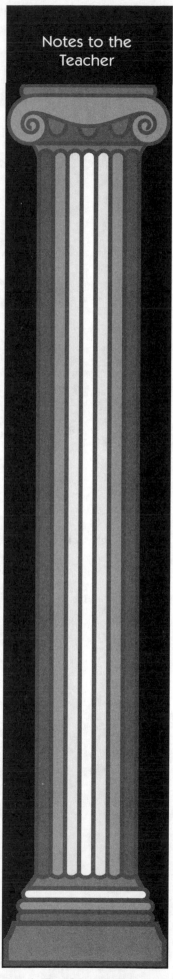
## Strategy Pages

**Strategy Pages** throughout the series have been developed to foster students' awareness of strategies that can be employed to increase understanding of literature. Some important examples are

- Monitoring (such as adjusting reading rate; consulting outside sources for further information; using context, including illustrations to help clarify meaning; rereading)
- Identifying important information (such as marking a text)
- Summarizing
- Evaluating
- Understanding the tools that writers use to make meaning—the elements of literature such as theme, plot, character, allusion, symbolism, metaphor

The focus of the pages for each literature selection reinforces the strategies important for engaging deeply with that particular work of literature.

## Testing

At the end of each group of 4 books, a comprehensive open-book **Test** has been provided for your use. Each test includes short essays that evoke a range of response types.

Answers are provided at the back of the book.

## Writer's Forum

Suggestions for writing are presented under the **Writer's Forum** heading throughout this guide. You can choose from these suggestions or substitute your own creative-writing ideas.

Each Writer's Forum includes both instruction and directions for a particular writing task using the writing process. Students will write in a variety of genres relating to the text and their own experience of the text. As you plan lessons, allow enough time for students to

- **Prewrite** (brainstorm and plan their work)
- **Draft** (give a shape to their ideas on paper)
- **Review** (revisit their work with an eye to improving it, on their own as well as with peers, with you, or with others)
- **Revise** (make changes that they feel will improve their draft)
- **Proofread** (check for accuracy in grammar, mechanics, and spelling)
- **Publish** (present their work to others in some way)

## Answer Pages

The **Answer Pages** contain brief answers or guidelines for the Journal and Discussion Topics, the Strategy Page questions, the Tests, and the Writer's Forum Page assignments. These answers are often not fully developed but suggest a starting place for evaluation of student work.

## INTRODUCING THE LITERATURE

Students will be better prepared to become involved with the work of literature if they can place it in a context. The process of **contextualizing** a work of literature begins with accessing their **prior knowledge** about the book, the author, the genre, and the subject. A class discussion is a good forum for this process. After you have found out what, if any, familiarity students have with

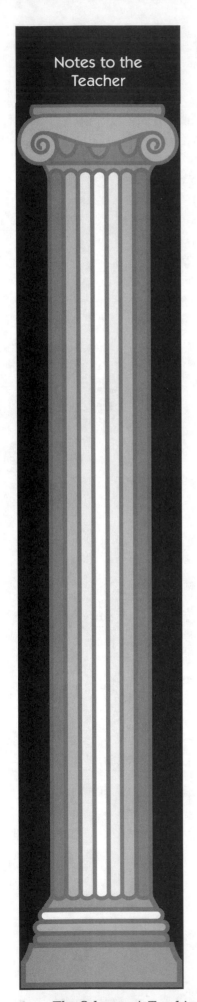

the book and author and what they have been able to discern about the genre and subject, you can provide any necessary background knowledge and, if it seems appropriate, correct any misapprehensions students have. See **Strategy 1: Beginning a Book**, pages 19–20.

Explain that in a work of fiction, an author creates an imaginary world. An important task in beginning a literature selection is to come to terms with that world. Point out that it is possible to consciously assess one's own understanding of literature and that this process is called **metacognitive reflection.** You may wish to model this process using a **think-aloud** approach as you go through the material on pages 19–20.

After students have a beginning notion of the context of a work, you can proceed with the prereading activities that students will use prior to every book.

### Sample Lesson Plan

Engaging **Prereading** activities include the following:
- Preview vocabulary and do a vocabulary exercise.
- Review the events of the previous book.
- Based on what you already know, examine your expectations about what will happen next, but be ready for surprises. Consider the book title and illustrations, if the text has them. If you wish, you can use a prediction guide. Students can fill in the guide as a class, in groups, or individually.

**During Reading,** students read with their Reader Response Journals. (You may wish to give them some of the journal and discussion topics before they read.)

Remind students of the questions that can help them to begin to understand a work of literature (see questions 7–10, page 20). You may wish to have students address these questions in their journals as they begin the book. Encourage students to continue using this kind of self-questioning in their Reader-Response Journals.

Additional journal activities they can use with every book include the following:
- A summary of the events of the book
- Evaluations of the characters and/or text
- Questions about what they have read
- Associations they have made between the text and other texts, experiences, or situations
- Notes on the images the text evoked
- Notes on the feelings the text evoked

**After Reading,** students complete the Journal and Discussion Topics, the Writer's Forum, the Strategy Pages, if any, and the Test.

As you and your students immerse yourselves in this work of literature, you may wish to consult other works by the same author, thematically related works, video and/or audio productions of the work, and criticism. (See the list of epics on page 11.) Here is a brief list of other works that may be useful:

Alexander, Lloyd. *The Arkadians.*

Cooper, Susan. *Over Sea, Under Stone.*

D'Aulaire, Ingri and Perin. *The Greek Myths.*

Homer. *The Iliad.* (many editions available—you may wish to choose one by the same translator you have for *The Odyssey*)

Jacques, Brian. *Redwall.*

Tolkien, J. R. R. *The Annotated Hobbit.*

Virgil. *The Aeneid.* (many editions available)

White, T. H. *The Sword in the Stone.*

**Note on the Spelling of Greek Proper Nouns in English:** Each of the 4 translators treated in this Literature Guide follows different rules for rendering Greek spelling into English. Except where the translations are treated separately on pages 21–25 (on which pages the spelling of the translation being discussed will be used), Fagles's spelling will be used throughout, because many people are still used to the Latinized versions of the Greek spellings. Thus, you will find *ch* instead of *kh*, *au* instead of *ao*, *ae* instead of *ai*, and *us* instead of *os* or *ös*. You will also see differences in the use of accents. Here is a chart of a few names so you can see the differences.

| **Fagles** | Telemachus | Menelaus | Achaeans | Antinous |
| **Fitzgerald** | Telémakhos | Meneláos | Achaians | Antinoös |
| **Lattimore** | Telemachos | Menelaos | Achaians | Antinoös |
| **Rouse** | Telemachos | Menelaos | Achaians | Antinoös |

The style of singular possessives for Greek names ending in *s*—an apostrophe only—used in the *Odyssey* translations is also used in this guide.

# STRATEGY 1 Genre—Epic

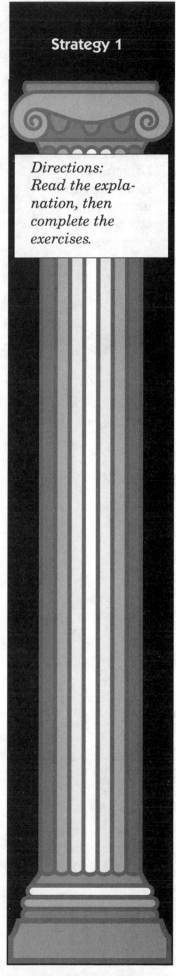

*Directions: Read the explanation, then complete the exercises.*

The word *epic* comes from the Greek word *epos* meaning "work," "narrative," or "song." An epic is a long narrative poem that recounts the adventures and heroic deeds of a real or legendary national hero. The earliest epics were works composed and recited orally and contain material that is considered mythical. The best-known of the early oral epics include *Gilgamesh* from ancient Sumer and the Greek national epics, the *Iliad* and the *Odyssey,* which are attributed to the poet Homer. Virgil's *Aeneid,* the first of the great literary epics, tells of the founding of Rome. Later epics from the medieval period and the Renaissance include the *Nibelungenlied* from Germany, *Jerusalem Delivered,* composed by the Italian poet Torquato Tasso, and two famous English epics, Edmund Spenser's *Faerie Queene* and John Milton's *Paradise Lost.* In modern times, oral epics continue to be composed, for example, by illiterate Slavic poets. People who perform epics are sometimes referred to as "minstrels" or "bards."

Epics composed orally differ from written epics in significant ways, as Walter J. Ong analyzes in his book, *Orality and Literacy.* Oral epics are composed in cultures that do not use a written language, referred to as "oral cultures." There are important differences in the way people think depending on whether or not they are literate, and some of the features of an oral culture show up in epic construction. For example, oral epics include mnemonic devices to help the bards remember the story. Written epics (or other stories) don't need such devices—the author, or the reader for that matter, can go back and reread to check on what happened previously. To assist their memories, the bards who composed oral epics included **formulas** phrases created to fit the poetic line (hexameter, in the case of Homer) that are repeated over and over—and **epithets**—phrases that characterize a thing or person and are used either with a proper name or in place of a proper name to fill up the poetic line. Writers tend to avoid such repetition and consider such phrases as overworked clichés.

Bards also use organizational techniques such as antitheses and standardized themes. They make use of sound patterns such as alliteration, assonance, and a strong rhythm. Some of these techniques help with memory; others make delivery of portions of the story automatic, so the poet can be thinking ahead to the next part.

1. Does the translation you are using render the *Odyssey* as poetry or prose? What rhythmic features can you identify?

2. Skim the book to identify some formulas and epithets. List them.

3. Does the translation you are using include instances of alliteration and assonance? Give some examples, if you find them.

4. Write a paragraph telling how you think life would be different for you if you could neither read nor write (besides the fact that you wouldn't be reading these directions).

# STRATEGY 2 Translations

Directions:
Read the explanation, then complete the exercises.

The *Odyssey* was composed nearly 3,000 years ago, and there have been many works composed subsequently that relate to it in various ways.

- **Translations** A translation is a rendering of a work created in one language into the words of a different language. A translation does not necessarily maintain the form of the original work (for example, poetry may be rendered as prose), and translators deal with issues such as idioms and syntax differently. But in any case, a translation is a fairly close and careful rendering of a work in a new language. The style used in a translation reflects something of the time in which it is written. Critics seem to feel that some translations come closer to the "spirit" of the original work than others.

- **Retellings** A retelling is a freer rendering than a translation. It transmits the story, but not sentence by sentence, line by line, as a translation does. This kind of rendering is true to the plot line of the story, but may not try to convey the particular color and flavor of the language and style found in the original work.

- **Adaptations** An adaptation is even looser than a retelling. A work is often adapted if it is being conveyed through a different medium. For example, to use the *Odyssey* as the basis of a television series, a ballet, a cartoon, a musical, or a computer game would require some adaptation of the story to fit the demands of the new medium.

1. Read the following excerpts from various renderings of the beginning of the *Odyssey* from Homeric Greek into English. Then answer the questions.

   **A.** The Man, O Muse, informe, that many a way
   Wound with his wisedome to his wished stay;
   That wanderd wondrous farre when He the towne
   Of sacred Troy had sackt and shiverd downe.
   The cities of a world of nations,
   With all their manners, mindes and fashions,
   He saw and knew; at Sea felt many woes,
   Much care sustaind, to save from overthrowes
   Himselfe and friends in their retreate for home.
   But so their fates he could not overcome,
   Though much he thirsted it. O men unwise,
   They perisht by their owne impieties,
   That in their hunger's rapine would not shunne
   The Oxen of the loftie-going Sunne,
   Who therefore from their eyes the day bereft
   Of safe returne. These acts, in some part left,
   Tell us, as others, deified seed of Jove.
   ~George Chapman

   **B.** This is the story of a man, one who was never at a loss. He had travelled far in the world, after the sack of Troy, the virgin fortress; he saw many cities of men, and learnt their mind; he endured many troubles and hardships in the struggle to save his own life and to bring back his men safe to their homes. He did his best, but he could not save his

companions. For they perished by their own madness, because they killed and ate the cattle of Hyperion the Sun-god, and the god took care that they should never see home again.
~ W. H. D. Rouse

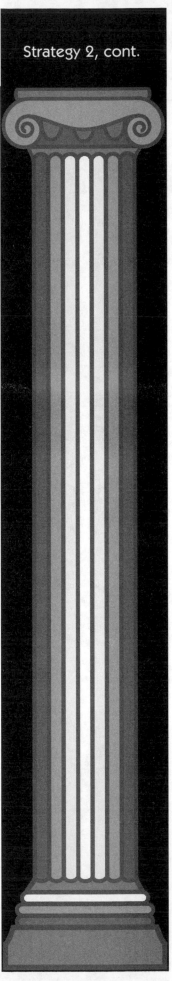

**C.** BILLY BLUE (*Sings*)
Gone sing 'bout that man because his stories please us,
Who saw trials and tempests for ten years after Troy.

I'm Blind Billy Blue, my main man's sea-smart Odysseus,
Who the God of the Sea drove crazy and tried to destroy.

Andra moi ennepe mousa polutropon hos mala polla . . .
The shuttle of the sea moves back and forth on this line,

All night, like the surf, she shuttles and doesn't fall
Asleep, then her rosy fingers at dawn unstitch the design.

When you hear this chord
(Chord)
                          Look for a swallow's wings,
A swallow arrowing seaward like a messenger

Passing smoke-blue islands, happy that the kings
Of Troy are going home and its ten years' siege is over.

So my blues drift like smoke from the fire of that war,
Cause once Achilles was ashes, things sure fell apart.

Slow-striding Achilles, who put the hex on Hector
A swallow twitters in Troy. That's where we start.
(*Exit.*)
~ Derek Walcott

**D.** Sing in me, Muse, and through me tell the story
of that man skilled in all ways of contending,
the wanderer, harried for years on end,
after he plundered the stronghold
on the proud height of Troy.

                          He saw the townlands
and learned the minds of many distant men,
and weathered many bitter nights and days
in his deep heart at sea, while he fought only
to save his life, to bring his shipmates home.
But not by will nor valor could he save them,
for their own recklessness destroyed them all—
children and fools, they killed and feasted on
the cattle of Lord Hêlios, the Sun,
and he who moves all day through heaven
took from their eyes the dawn of their return.
~ Robert Fitzgerald

**E.** Tell me, Muse, of the man of many ways, who was driven
far journeys, after he had sacked Troy's sacred citadel.
Many were they whose cities he saw, whose minds he learned of,
many the pains he suffered in his spirit on the wide sea,
struggling for his own life and the homecoming of his companions.
Even so he could not save his companions, hard though

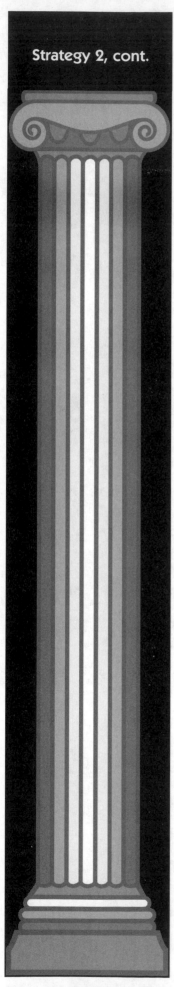

he strove to; they were destroyed by their own wild recklessness,
fools, who devoured the oxen of Helios, the Sun God,
and he took away the day of their homecoming.
        ~Richmond Lattimore

F.      The story of the siege of Troy I have already told in another book.
That was the story of how golden Helen left her husband, Menelaus,
the King of Sparta, to go with Prince Paris to his home in Troy; and
how the black ships gathered from all the kingdoms and the islands of
Greece at the summons of Agamemnon, the High King, and sailed to
conquer the city and bring Helen back.

The siege lasted for nine years, and many great heroes both Greek
and Trojan died in the fighting before all was done.  But at last, by a
cunning device of Odysseus, King of Ithaca (not for nothing did men
call him Odysseus the Resourceful), a Greek war-band was smuggled
inside the city, hidden in the hollow belly of a huge wooden horse.  And
in the dark of night they opened the city gates and let their comrades in.
        ~Rosemary Sutcliff

G.  Sing to me of the man, Muse, the man of twists and turns
driven time and again off course, once he had plundered
the hallowed heights of Troy.
Many cities of men he saw and learned their minds,
many pains he suffered, heartsick on the open sea,
fighting to save his life and bring his comrades home.
But he could not save them from disaster, hard as he strove—
the recklessness of their own ways destroyed them all,
the blind fools, they devoured the cattle of the Sun
and the Sungod blotted out the day of their return.
        ~Robert Fagles

1.  Identify each of the renderings as a translation, retelling, or adaptation.
    Give a reason for your answer.

2.  Which of the renderings do you like best, and why?

3.  One of these renditions was composed in 1614–1615.  Which one do you
    think it is?  What leads you to think as you do?

4.  What similarities and differences do you find between **B, D, E,** and **G?**

# STRATEGY 3

## Background—The Historical Troy

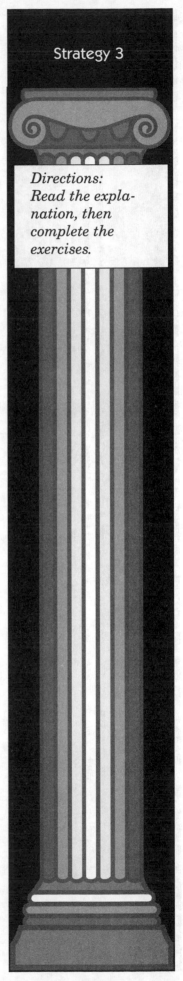

*Directions: Read the explanation, then complete the exercises.*

The man who is largely responsible for our historical knowledge of Troy and verification of historical details in Homer's works was fascinated by Homer from the time he was a child. When he wrote the book telling the world that he had actually discovered the ancient city of Troy, he began like this: "When, in the year 1832 . . . at the age of ten, I presented my father, as a Christmas gift, with a badly written Latin essay upon the principal events of the Trojan war and the adventures of Ulysses [the Latin name for Odysseus] and Agamemnon, little did I think that, six-and-thirty years later, I should offer the public a work on the same subject, after having had the good fortune to see with my own eyes the scene of that war, and the country of the heroes whose names have been immortalized by Homer." This man's name was Heinrich Schliemann, and the archaeological dig he began at the site that is now known as Hissarlik, Turkey, is believed to have really uncovered the city of Troy mentioned in Homer's works.

Schliemann explored the site at Hissarlik from 1870 to 1890, and his work was continued after his death by Wilhelm Dorpfeld (1893–1894). Later, in the 1930s, the site was reviewed by a team led by Carl W. Blegen. The work of these archaeologists revealed that the fortress and city of Troy existed from about 3000 B.C. to 1100 B.C. in a series of seven major settlements. Two later settlements occurred after 700 B.C. The first two settlements, Troy I and Troy II, were both destroyed in great fires. Troy VI was destroyed by an earthquake, and the survivors built Troy VIIa which lasted from about 1300–1200 B.C. Troy VIIa is the settlement that is believed to be the focus of the action in the *Iliad* and the site of the war from which Odysseus was returning in the *Odyssey.*

What leads people to believe this? First, tradition holds that the fall of Troy occurred in 1184 B.C., and this date matches the approximate date of the end of the settlement. Second, Schliemann found other evidence that points to Troy VIIa as the site referred to in Homer and recorded it in his book. Finds such as helmet crests made with a ridge on which to fix a horse-hair plume, as mentioned in the *Iliad,* convinced Schliemann that he had truly found Troy. He said in his book, "Now as regards the results of my excavations, everyone must admit that I have solved a great historical problem, and that I have solved it by the discovery of a high civilization . . . in the depths of an ancient town, which throughout antiquity was called Ilium and declared itself to be the successor of Troy, the site of which was regarded as identical with the site of the Homeric Ilium by the whole civilized world of that time. The situation of this town not only corresponds perfectly with all the statements of the *Iliad,* but also with all the traditions handed down to us by later authors; and, moreover, neither in the Plain of Troy, nor in its vicinity, is there any other place which could in the slightest degree be made to correspond to them."

## Background—A Brief History of the Trojan War

After Paris (the son of Priam, king of Troy) elopes with Helen (wife of Menelaus, king of Sparta), Menelaus' countrymen (the Greeks or Achaeans) join him in his plan to get Helen back. Menelaus' brother, Agamemnon, high king of Argos is to be the commander in chief of the Achaean army. Odysseus, prince of Ithaca—who has recently married Penelope and has a young son, Telemachus—does not want to leave home, so he pretends to be mad. When Palamedes is sent to urge him to join his countrymen, Odysseus yokes an ox and an ass together and begins to plow a field with this ungainly pair, sowing

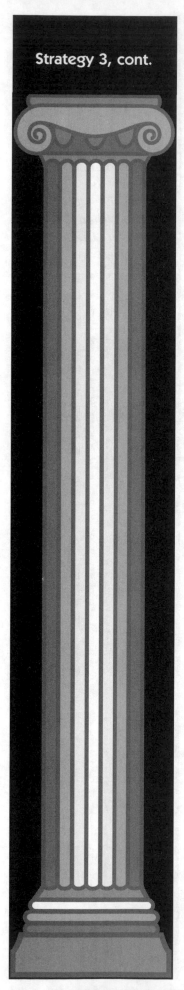

salt instead of seeds. Palamedes places baby Telemachus before the plow, and Odysseus proves his sanity by stopping so that he will not hurt his son. Odysseus is persuaded to honor his oath of loyalty to Menelaus, as all the other princes chose to do, and join the army.

After 2 years of preparation, the Achaean fleet sets sail. The Trojans oppose their landing, but the Achaeans are able to encamp and lay siege to Troy. For 9 years the battle is not decisive. In the tenth year, when the *Iliad* takes place, the Achaean prince and their greatest warrior, Achilles, kills the Trojan hero Hector, another of Priam's sons. This is where the tale of the *Iliad* ends. Achilles is then slain by Paris.

The Achaeans discover that Troy cannot be defeated without the arrows and bow of Hercules, both of which are now owned by Philoctetes. But the Achaeans had left Philoctetes on the island of Lemnos on the way to Troy, because he had a wound in his foot and his cries of pain were unbearable to his fellow sailors. Achilles' son, Neoptolemus, and Odysseus travel to Lemnos and bring Philoctetes and the weapons of Hercules to Troy, where Philoctetes (or Neoptolemus, depending on which version you read) uses the bow to kill Paris. But still they cannot take the citadel. Odysseus and Diomedes steal a statue of Athena, called the Palladium, from Troy, with Helen's secret help (for by now, she wants to return home to Menelaus), after learning that Troy cannot be taken as long as the statue remains inside the walls. And still they cannot prevail.

Finally, the Achaeans decide to use a trick, some stories say at Odysseus' suggestion. They build an enormous wooden horse, which they pretend is an offering to the goddess Athena, and they leave it before the gates of Troy. Then they go to their ships, embark, and pretend to depart. However, the horse is actually filled with armed soldiers. The Trojans — ignoring the advice of Laocoön, the priest of Poseidon, to beware of Greek gifts — take the horse into the city. Under cover of night, the Greeks come out of the horse, open the gates of the city to admit their fellow Achaeans, set fire to the city, and kill many of the Trojans, including King Priam. Helen returns to Menelaus, and the Achaeans depart for home. But because the princess Cassandra, daughter of Priam, is abused by the Achaeans at the war's end, Athena becomes angry with the Greeks, and makes their homecomings difficult. For example, it takes Odysseus 10 years to get home. The *Odyssey* recounts the final portion of Odysseus' homeward journey, estimated by one scholar to be a period of about 6 weeks. It can be viewed as a sequel to the *Iliad*.

1. What criteria did Schliemann use to determine whether or not his dig corresponded to the legendary city known as Troy?

2. Make a timeline showing the sequence of events in the Trojan War.

# STRATEGY 4 Homer's Mythology

**Myths** are fundamental stories of a culture that explain basic principles, practices, beliefs, and/or traditions under which the culture operates. Myths tell the stories of the gods, goddesses, and heroes of the culture. They tell about the creation of the world, the origin of natural phenomena, the culture's rituals and ceremonies, and the reasons for specific characteristics of peoples and animals. Myths may also present a view of the afterlife.

*Mythology* is a word used to refer to the body of myths of a particular culture. Greek mythology is the collected myths of the ancient Greeks. Greek mythology is complicated in that the stories were recorded over a period of nearly 2,000 years and incorporate elements from unique local beliefs and customs as well as from several different traditions. In addition, the myths were used as material by all 3 great Greek tragedians (Euripides, Sophocles, and Aeschylus), by the poets Hesiod and Homer, and by some of the Greek philosophers, and the details in the different renditions sometimes conflict. To further convolute matters, the Romans recorded and reinterpreted Greek mythology (as in Virgil's *Aeneid*), changing the names of many of the gods as well as other details. In fact, many of the tales of the Greek myths come to us through the Latin work by Ovid called *Metamorphoses*.

*Directions: Read the explanation, then complete the exercises.*

As a result, when you are reading Homer and check a name in a source such as a mythological dictionary, you may find an entry that doesn't exactly match what you've read. How many Sirens were there? Is Scylla's mother Hecate or Cratais? Was Oedipus' mother Epicaste or Jocasta? Was the Trojan horse Odysseus' idea or not?

1. As you read, keep track of information in the *Odyssey* that matches or doesn't match other sources of Greek mythology.

## Who's Who in Homer's Mythology

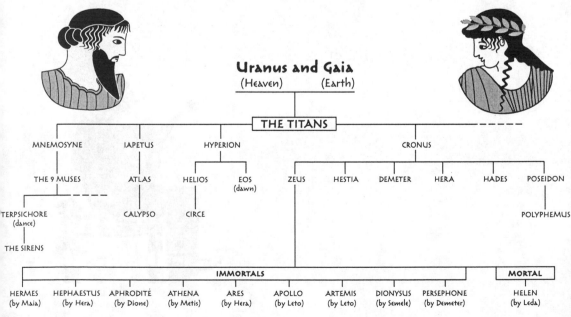

N.B. Helios is the son of Hyperion. But Homer calls Helios by the epithet *Hyperion*.

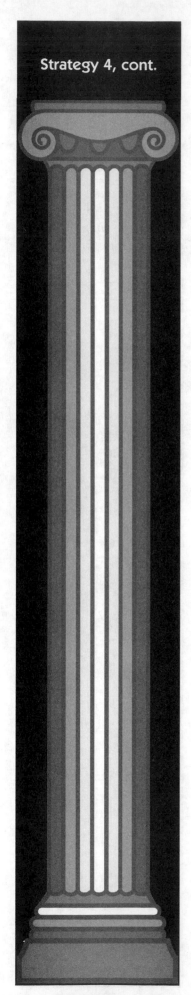

| | |
|---|---|
| Aphrodite | goddess of love and beauty |
| Apollo | god of medicine and music |
| Ares | god of war |
| Artemis | goddess of the hunt |
| Athena | goddess of wisdom, war, and weaving |
| Atlas | titan; he supports the sky |
| Calypso | goddess/nymph |
| Circe | goddess of the island of Aiaia |
| Cronus | titan; son of Heaven and Earth |
| Demeter | goddess of the harvest and grain |
| Dionysus | god of wine |
| Eos | goddess who brings the day; also called Dawn |
| Hades | god of the underworld |
| Helen | cause of the Trojan War; wife of Menelaus |
| Helios | god of the sun |
| Hephaestus | god of craftsmen and fire |
| Hera | queen of the gods, wife of Zeus |
| Hermes | Zeus' messenger |
| Hestia | goddess of the hearth |
| Hyperion | the original sun god |
| Mnemosyne | goddess of memory |
| Muses | nine goddesses of the arts: Calliope (epics), Clio (history), Erato (lyrics), Euterpe (music), Melpomene (tragedy), Poly-hymnia (hymns), Terpsichore (dance), Thalia (comedy), Urania (astronomy) |
| Persephone | queen of the dead |
| Polyphemus | greatest of the Cyclops |
| Poseidon | god of the sea |
| Sirens | creatures whose singing is irresistible |
| Zeus | king of the gods |

# STRATEGY 5        Beginning a Book

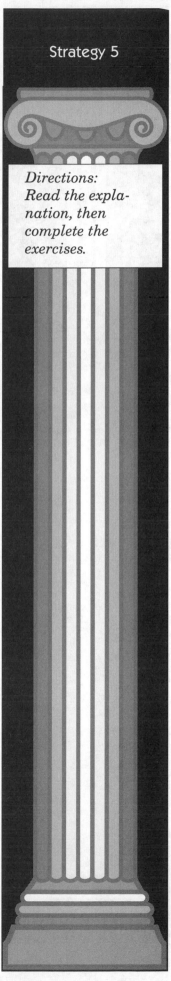

*Directions: Read the explanation, then complete the exercises.*

An artist or craftworker about to create a work chooses from a set of tools, techniques, and products. A photographer, for example, may have lenses of various shapes and sizes, film that is either color or black and white, and a 35-mm, 16-mm, or panoramic camera. The product may be a portrait, a landscape, a series of prints, or a work with several prints superimposed on each other. And the techniques used may include adjusting the film speed, using a colored lens or a lens with a special effect such as a wide-angle lens, or tinting a black and white photograph. In addition, there are certain conventions, such as expected angles and light settings, that the photographer may choose to employ or not. The photographer does not use every technique and material in every photograph, and the photographer's choices are guided by the artistic goal, which might be the answer to a question such as, "How can I effectively communicate my vision?" The viewer coming to see the finished product can examine the techniques and materials as they are manifested there. Moving closer and further away, attending to detail, shape, color, angle, and the effect of the whole, the viewer can come to understand the photograph.

The writer is an artist who works in words that create images, thoughts, and feelings in the reader. Like the photographer, the writer usually isn't there when the reader experiences the product (in this case a book), but reading is, nevertheless, an act of communication. Like the photographer, the writer works to communicate a vision to people who are not present. The reader's understanding of the tools, techniques, products, and conventions of writing helps the reader to understand the vision. But at the same time that we try to understand the writer's communication, we must acknowledge that each reader also brings an individual and unique understanding to the act of reading, and so no 2 readers will experience a book in exactly the same way; different readers will have different insights and feelings, so discussion between and among readers can enrich the experience of all.

Beginning a book is particularly important, because readers starting a book are entering a new and uncharted territory. When you are starting a book, paying particular attention to the writer's use of tools, techniques, and conventions can help.

**TITLE** The title of the book—found on the front cover, the spine, and the title page—may explicitly tell what the book is about, hint at the story, or seem very mysterious. Depending on the title, you may feel interested, curious, hopeful, etc. The author's name follows immediately after the title. If you know anything about the author—for example, that Homer was an Ancient Greek bard who composed his work orally—it might help you make predictions about the content of the book.

**COVER ILLUSTRATION** Most books have a picture on the cover. The writer may or may not have had a voice in what appears, so the illustration may not represent the writer's vision. Nevertheless, it can give you some idea of characters, setting, and plot in the story.

**COPYRIGHT PAGE** The copyright page tells the dates of the book's publication. Since translations reflect both the original work and the culture of the time in which they were created, this can be important for editions of the *Odyssey*.

**OTHER BOOKS BY** Sometimes there is a list before the title page that names other books by the same author. If you are familiar with, say, the *Iliad*,

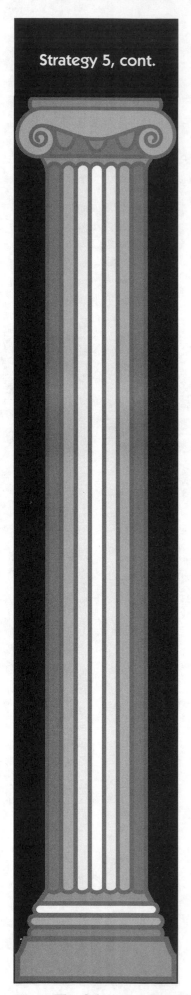

you may have some idea of what to expect in the *Odyssey*. This is also true if you have heard about the book from friends, read a book review, heard the book on audiotape, or seen a movie version. This is some of your prior knowledge about the book you are about to read.

**TABLE OF CONTENTS** While some books have unnamed divisions, sometimes authors title their chapters or sections. Like the book title, these titles may reveal more or less about what happens in the book.

**INSIDE ILLUSTRATIONS** Some books are illustrated throughout with drawings, paintings, photographs, etc. None of the 4 versions of Homer has these. Fagles's version includes 3 maps and 4 genealogical diagrams.

**BACK COVER BLURB** The note on the back cover is advertising, meant to give away enough of the story to pique your interest and convince you to buy the book. In the case of the *Odyssey,* it focuses on the comparative qualities of the translation, rather than on the plot of the epic.

**FIRST FEW PARAGRAPHS** The first few pages of the text provide the writer with the first opportunity to introduce the story. Read carefully to learn as much as you can about the world of the book.

1.  What is your reaction to the title of the book?

2.  Describe the cover illustration. What can you gather from it?

3.  How long has it been since this book was first published?

4.  What, if anything, do you already know about Homer, his works, or the *Odyssey?*

5.  What can you tell about the story from the book title and/or descriptions?

6.  Read to line 20 (to the end of the second paragraph in Rouse). Who seem(s) to be the most important character(s)? How can you tell?

7.  Finish Book 1. Where does the story take place? What special characteristics does the setting have?

8.  What themes does the story seem to have so far?

9.  What do you predict will happen next in the story?

10. What more do you want to know about the setting and the characters?

# INTRODUCTION TO THE TRANSLATION OF
# Robert Fagles

## Notes to the Teacher

The apparatus accompanying the Fagles translation includes

- an Introduction and Notes by classicist Bernard Knox,
- a guide to pronunciation,
- three maps,
- a Translator's Postscript,
- genealogies for the main characters,
- Suggestions for Further Reading, and
- a Pronouncing Glossary.

The glossary, maps, and genealogies may help students while they are reading the *Odyssey* for the first time. The Introduction will "give away" the story, and so you may want to reserve consideration of its main points for a time after students have finished reading the text. Details about the translation, from both the Introduction and the Translator's Postscript, might be useful for students to know as they read.

Here are the main points: Fagles has translated the Oxford University edition of the Greek text edited by David Monro and Thomas Allen (1908), but not with a line-by-line translation. He uses either a 5- or a 6-beat line, and occasionally increases or decreases the count to render a certain meaning. He varies the translation of standard epithets to reflect the context, but for longer passages of repeated material, he repeats the translation "closely."

## Journal and Discussion Topics

### Introduction

1. Bernard Knox sets himself questions several times in his essay. For each question, identify the answer(s) that Knox gives.
   a. (page 3) How did the *Odyssey* survive for 2,700 years?
   b. (page 3) How was the *Odyssey* composed?
   c. (page 3) Who wrote the *Odyssey* and for what audience?
2. According to Knox, how are the *Odyssey* and the *Iliad* related?
3. What, according to Knox, does Odysseus want most?
4. What does Knox identify as the theme of the *Odyssey*? How is it revealed?
5. On what grounds does Knox compare and contrast Odysseus and Achilles?
6. Why is the punishment of the Phaecians ironic, according to Knox?
7. How does Knox characterize Telemachus' attitude toward his mother?
8. How does Knox explain Penelope's sudden decision to marry?
9. What defenses does Knox offer for the authenticity of Book 24?

### Homeric Geography

1. Explain the geographical relationships among the 3 maps.
2. Where is Ithaca on the second map? Where would it be if it appeared on the third?
3. About how far would you have to travel if you were sailing as directly as possible from Troy to Ithaca?

**Translation of Robert Fagles, cont.**

### Translator's Postscript

1. How does Fagles's treatment of epithets differ from his treatment of longer repetitions? What is his rationale for this differentiation?
2. What factors influence the length of Fagles's English line?
3. What kind of help did Fagles have in making his translation?
4. How, according to Fagles, does Odysseus' journey continue?

### The Genealogies

1. What's the relationship between Odysseus and Zeus?
2. Autolycus' father was the god Hermes, which makes Hermes what relation to Odysseus?
3. What relationship are Arete and Alcinous to each other?
4. How is Poseidon related to Nausicaa? To Nestor?

# INTRODUCTION TO THE TRANSLATION OF
# Robert Fitzgerald

## Notes to the Teacher

The apparatus accompanying the Fitzgerald translation includes a Postscript by the translator.

You might consider having students read Fitzgerald's discussion of his translation (the last 2 pages of the postscript, pages 508–509) before they begin the text of the *Odyssey*, so that they understand **his** understanding of his art. The rest you may wish to save until after they have completed the book. If possible, share the pronunciation guide from another edition with students, so they have a reference for the many Greek names of people and places.

## Journal and Discussion Topics

### Postscript

1. What does Fitzgerald gather from the geographical mistakes he makes?
2. How does Fitzgerald reason out the action of Agamemnon when he hears Kassandra cry?
3. How does Fitzgerald imagine the contest of the bow?
4. Draw a sketch to match Fitzgerald's explanation of the layout of the entryway.
5. What is Fitzgerald's rationale for his use of the word *falcon*?
6. How was the *Odyssey* composed, according to Fitzgerald?
7. What kind of performance does Fitzgerald imagine the *Odyssey* had in Homer's day?
8. If you had the task of dividing the *Odyssey* into sections, how would you group the books and why?
9. How does Fitzgerald characterize the relationship between the *Iliad* and the *Odyssey?*
10. How does Fitzgerald explain Penelope's actions in Books XVII–XXIII?
11. What proof does Fitzgerald give that Book XXIV is integral to the rest of the text?
12. Fitzgerald discusses the importance of "self-mastery" in the *Odyssey.* What do you see as the importance of "self-mastery" in the *Odyssey?*

**Translation of Richmond Lattimore**

# Richmond Lattimore

## Notes to the Teacher

The apparatus accompanying the Lattimore translation includes

- an Introduction by the translator and
- a Pronouncing Glossary.

In his Note on the Translation at the end of the Introduction, Lattimore refers the reader to his principles of translation as stated in his Note on the Translation of the *Iliad.* You may wish to read this passage (about three-quarters of a page, page 55) to students. In summary, he says that his goal is to translate the meaning with English in "a speed and rhythm analogous" to the Greek text. He uses a free 6-beat line, and (as he implies in the Introduction to the *Iliad*) he repeats verbatim when Homer does. You may wish to have students finish the book before reading the Introduction. Students will find the Pronouncing Glossary to be a useful reference as they read.

## Journal and Discussion Topics
### Introduction

1. What do you think of Lattimore's division of the *Odyssey* into sections? Explain your reasoning.
2. If you had the task of summarizing the *Odyssey,* how would your summary differ from Lattimore's?
3. What is gained, according to Lattimore, by beginning with the Telemachy?
4. How does Lattimore divide the Wanderings?
5. Does Lattimore view the world of the Wanderings as real or imaginary?
6. On what grounds does Lattimore argue that the Wanderings are not symbolic?
7. Did your impression as you read the 9 books between Odysseus' arrival in Ithaka and his attack on the suitors match Lattimore's (page 16) or not? Explain.
8. Do you find the doom of the suitors "excessive"? Why or why not?
9. What evidence supports the end of the *Odyssey* as authentic, in Lattimore's view?
10. What evidence does Lattimore give to support the concept of a single composer for both the *Iliad* and the *Odyssey?*

# INTRODUCTION TO THE TRANSLATION OF
# W. H. D. Rouse

## Notes to the Teacher
The apparatus accompanying the Rouse translation includes

- John Keats's poem "On First Looking into Chapman's Homer,"
- a Preface by the translator
- an essay entitled "Homer's Words," and
- a Pronouncing Index.

Rouse's intention is to capture the simplicity and naturalness of Homer's style and language. He conveys this in the brief preface and in the first few pages (272–278) of his essay on Homer's Words. You may wish to have students refer to these to get a sense of the translator's aims before beginning the text. There is a lot of Greek in the essay, most of it translated. Pointing this out to students may help them not to be overwhelmed by the appearance of an essay with so many foreign words. (The end of the translator's essay can be saved until after the students have finished the text.) You may wish to use Keats's poem in connection with Rouse's comments on translation in speaking about the role of the translator. While they read, students will find the Pronouncing Index useful.

## Journal and Discussion Topics
### "On First Looking into Chapman's Homer"
1. Keats wrote this poem in October, 1816, after reading George Chapman's translation of the *Iliad*. Restate the poem in your own words in prose.
2. What do you think the adjective "deep-browed" is intended to convey (line 6)?
3. Keats made a mistake concerning an historical occurrence in this poem. Can you discover what it is and supply the correct information?
4. Have you ever been profoundly influenced by a work of literature? Describe your reaction to a work that you found particularly moving, important, influential, or exciting.

### Preface
1. What problem did Rouse find with the translations of Homer available in his day?
2. How does Rouse defend the "simple style" he employs in his translation?

### Homer's Words
1. What distinguishes "natural" and literary style, according to Rouse?
2. What does Rouse say characterizes Homer's
   a. forms,
   b. words, and
   c. stock epithets?
3. How, according to Rouse, do Homer's words and style relate to speech in Greece in Homer's day?

# Book 1

## Journal and Discussion Topics

1. How do the gods make decisions?
2. How do the gods interact with people? What seem to be the limits of their "interference" with people's lives?
3. How do you interpret Telemachus' response to Athena's/Mentes' comment that Telemachus looks like Odysseus?
4. Explain Telemachus' dilemma in your own words.
5. What practical advice does Athena/Mentes give Telemachus?
6. What model does Athena/Mentes propose that Telemachus follow?
7. How do you feel about the exchange between Penelope and Telemachus? Explain why you feel as you do.
8. What would you do if you were in Telemachus' situation? In Penelope's situation? If you were Athena?
9. What struck you most in this book?
10. What part of this book was easiest for you to visualize?
11. What do you predict will happen in the rest of the story? What evidence supports your predictions?
12. In general, when we read poetry, we are careful to distinguish the speaker from the poet. How do you think we might understand the relationship of speaker and poet in oral/performed poetry?

## Summary

The speaker/poet/performer introduces the story by invoking the Muse to help him convey the tale of the unnamed protagonist. This resourceful man went through great struggles as he tried to make his way home after the fall of Troy at the end of the Trojan War. Although he tried to save them, all his companions were lost through their own fault, because they ate Helios' cattle. The protagonist is presently a prisoner on the island of the deity Calypso, during the year in which he is fated to return home to Ithaca.

It was the wrath of Poseidon that kept the man, Odysseus, from his home, but now, taking advantage of Poseidon's absence in Ethiopia, Athena recalls for Zeus the plight of Odysseus, and Zeus says that Poseidon must join with the majority in allowing Odysseus' homecoming. Athena asks that Hermes be sent to Ogygia to tell Calypso that Odysseus must be allowed to depart. In the meantime, Athena will go to Ithaca to hearten Telemachus so that he will warn the suitors and begin a search for his father, in the process earning support for himself.

Disguised as a family friend, Mentes, Athena comes to the house of Odysseus and finds the suitors entertaining themselves and waiting for a meal. [We will refer to Athena as Mentes while she appears as him.] Telemachus greets "Mentes" with great courtesy and sees that he is well cared for. After the meal, when the harpist begins to sing, however, Telemachus whispers to Mentes the substance of his problem—the suitors are living in Odysseus' house and eating up the property; but if the owner were to return, they could not run away quickly enough to escape his wrath. Then he asks for Mentes' name and history. Mentes tells of the connection between his family and that of Odysseus. He says clearly that

Odysseus is not dead, but only detained, and that Odysseus will soon return to Ithaca. Telemachus tells how the lords of Ithaca and the nearby islands are courting his mother, who hates the thought of marriage to any of them yet dares not send them away. Mentes gives Telemachus the following advice: first, to call an assembly the following day and say before all that the suitors should leave the house; second, to go in search of news of his father; third, to return and consider how to kill the suitors, following the example set by Orestes. Mentes insists on returning to his ship without the gifts that Telemachus wishes to bestow on him, telling Telemachus to save them for another time. He leaves like a bird, which reveals to Telemachus that a god has been with him.

Penelope enters, as the minstrel continues singing, and asks him to choose a different tale because his song of the homecoming of the Greeks grieves her. Telemachus interrupts and dismisses her, saying she has no reason to criticize the minstrel. When she retires to cry herself to sleep, Telemachus, following Mentes' advice, warns the suitors that he will call the assembly in the morning and send them from the house. One of the suitors, Antinous, insults Telemachus and prays to Zeus that Telemachus will never be king of Ithaca. Telemachus answers that he would be king if Zeus willed it, but for now he only wants to rule his own house. Eurymachus agrees that Telemachus should be the ruler in his own house and asks about the stranger. Telemachus says that his guest was a family friend, Mentes, not revealing that he knows it was a god in disguise. After the suitors leave for the night, Telemachus is helped to bed by Eurycleia, his nurse, who is devoted to him, and he spends the night thinking of Athena's advice.

Book 1, cont.

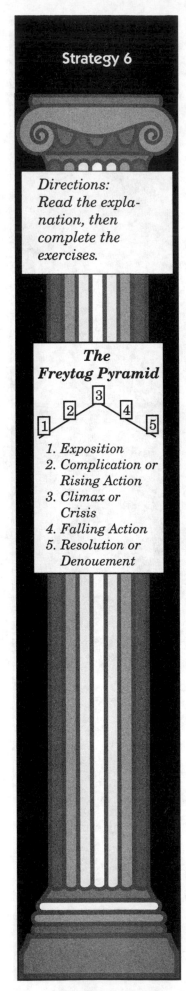

Directions: Read the explanation, then complete the exercises.

**The Freytag Pyramid**

1. Exposition
2. Complication or Rising Action
3. Climax or Crisis
4. Falling Action
5. Resolution or Denouement

# STRATEGY 6

## Plot—Beginning/Middle/End

Every story has a **plot** or sequence of actions. People who study literature have come up with several different ways of talking about plot. When people talk about stories with young children, they often refer to the beginning, the middle, and the end. This is not just a notion for little kids. These 3 parts are the way screenwriters and television writers arrange their scripts. Dramatists, on the other hand, often work with a 5-act play. Each of the 5 acts represents an essential and sequential part of the drama. Narrative is also often presented in high school and college classes as having these 5 parts:

1. **Exposition**—introduction of essential background information, as well as characters, situations, and conflicts. Exposition may be found throughout a story, as well as at the beginning.

2. **Complication**—the beginning of the central conflict in the story.

3. **Crisis**—(sometimes called the **turning point**) usually the point at which the main character's action or choice determines the outcome of the conflict. Or, **Climax:** the high point of the action.

4. **Falling Action**—the time when all the pieces fall into place and the ending becomes inevitable

5. **Resolution or Denouement**—the conflicts are resolved and the story is concluded.

But this well-known structure is not followed in the *Odyssey,* if we consider it as the story of Odysseus' homecoming. The *Odyssey* starts in the middle of things, what the Roman poet, Horace, refers to as *in media res.* The concept of beginning, middle, and end are different from what you might expect for several reasons. First, the audience for whom Homer was performing knew the background of the story intimately (from the *Iliad,* as well as from other sources). Second, the audience knew the entire story, including the end, before the performer started singing. So the performer did not use suspense (the building up of expectation about things unknown) in the same way as when a story is a new invention that the audience doesn't know. Likewise, the bard didn't use much situational irony—the kind of irony in which the situation that unfolds in the story is contrary to what we expect. (See Strategy 15, page 72, for more on irony.) And, possibly because this was an oral composition, and the poet did not have access to writing to organize his ideas, the oral poet didn't necessarily use Freytag's pyramid, which shows dramatic development from beginning, through the middle, and to the end of a story that is told primarily in chronological order.

The oral performer concentrates on other aspects of storytelling to engage the audience, such as **elaboration** (the filling in of interesting details and background) and **repetitions and parallels** that show the similarities and differences in situations, attitudes, etc. **Delay** is another tactic—the audience knows what will happen but not exactly when and how.

Consider these questions as you read, and answer them when you have sufficient information.

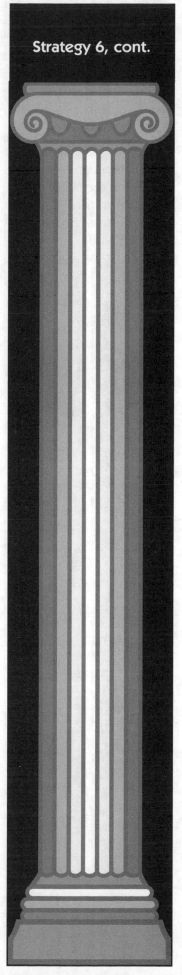

1. Describe the organization of the *Odyssey* in your own words.

2. As you read the *Odyssey,* create a graphic in which you rearrange the events so that you understand what happened to Odysseus in chronological order.

3. Analyze the results of your answer to numbers 1 and 2. What would be gained if a performer presented the story in chronological order? What would be lost?

4. Find instances of elaboration in the *Odyssey.* What do they add to the experience of the reader?

5. Find instances of repetitions and parallels in the *Odyssey.* How does Homer use them to make meaning?

6. Are there times in the *Odyssey* when you feel that Homer is delaying? Identify one or more and explain.

# STRATEGY 7 References and Allusions— The Story of Agamemnon

A **reference** is a mention of something outside the work you are currently reading. It could be a reference to a real or imaginary event, person, or place; or to another literary work (often in a quotation), an aspect of culture, or a fact. References are often documented.

An **allusion** is an *indirect* reference—one that you need to recognize as a reference without the author telling you that it is one. After you recognize the allusion, you need to figure out what it means in the context. Sometimes an author will include clues like quotation marks, or introductory words (as the great philosopher once said . . .), or use a name. But sometimes, especially if recognizing and understanding it are not essential to the author's point or if the author assumes that virtually every reader will recognize the allusion, the author may not signal the allusion. S/he may, instead, rely on readers sharing a common knowledge of literature, history, biography, science, and art that in most cases will help readers figure out meanings. Sometimes allusions can be like private jokes, inserted for those who can get them. Allusions help the reader see the work as part of a greater literary tradition.

Many references and allusions support or reinforce the meaning in the text. But this is not their only possible purpose. References and allusions can provide contrasts as well as parallels. In the *Odyssey,* Homer uses the story of Agamemnon's homecoming as a counterpoint to his story of Odysseus' homecoming. The various mentions of Agamemnon sometimes have more, sometimes less explanation. Here is a brief account to help you understand the use Homer is making of this story that was so well-known to his audience.

Helen was the wife of Menelaus, and Paris, the son of King Priam of Troy, took her away to Troy. Agamemnon, the brother of Menelaus, was the High King of Argos and he prepared to lead the Achaean troops to Troy to bring back Helen. Lacking a wind to sail by, the Achaeans consulted a seer who said that Agamemnon had offended Artemis who demanded a sacrifice—Agamemnon's daughter Iphigenia. Agamemnon completed the sacrifice, and the wind took the Achaean ships to Troy.

But Clytemnestra (Agamemnon's wife and Iphigenia's mother) could not forgive Agamemnon for Iphigenia's death. She took Aegisthus, Agamemnon's cousin whom Agamemnon had robbed of the throne, as her lover, and planned to avenge the death of Iphigenia by killing Agamemnon. Clytemnestra and Aegisthus murdered Agamemnon shortly after he returned home from Troy. Years later, when Orestes, the son of Agamemnon and Clytemnestra, was grown, he killed both Aegisthus and Clytemnestra in revenge.

1. Keep a record of the references and allusions in the text to the story of Agamemnon. For each occasion, note the following:

   • Where does the mention occur? Who makes it?
   • Would you consider this a reference or an allusion? Why?
   • What is the relationship between the mention and the story of Odysseus? Are they identical or parallel? Or is Homer using them to point to a contrast?
   • What is the point of bringing up Agamemnon's story in the particular context? Is it told as part of the history of the Greek heroes, as a demonstration of a moral point, etc.?

# Book 2

## Journal and Discussion Topics

1. What does the role of the Council seem to be in Ithaca?
2. Whose responsibility do you think it is that the suitors continue to pursue Penelope and use up the substance of Odysseus' house? Explain your reasoning.
3. If you heard a man give a speech and he began crying, what would you think of him? What do you make of the crowd's reaction to Telemachus?
4. If you were Telemachus, what would you say to Penelope?
5. Describe the manner in which each person listed below speaks. What can you conclude about them?
   - Telemachus
   - Eurymachus
   - Halitherses
   - Antinous
   - Mentor
6. How do the members of the Council respond to Telemachus' final request?
7. List all the deceptions that you find mentioned in this book.
8. What does Eurycleia say to try to persuade Telemachus not to travel?
9. What does Athena do to help Telemachus?
10. What do you think the suitors will do while Telemachus is gone?

## Summary

Telemachus rises at dawn and tells the criers to call the Achaeans to assembly. Lord Aegyptius opens the meeting by asking who has called the assembly and for what reason. Telemachus answers him, explaining the situation with the suitors. He ends by throwing down the speaker's staff with tears in his eyes. Antinous rebukes Telemachus and blames Penelope for the situation, describing how she tricked the suitors by telling them she would marry when she finished weaving a shroud for Odysseus' father, Laertes, but secretly unraveled her work at night so that it would never be finished. Telemachus replies that he can't banish his mother, and he tells the suitors that if they don't leave, he will pray for Zeus' vengeance to come upon them. When he says this, Zeus sends 2 eagles that drop into the crowd, tearing with their talons. Halitherses, a man skilled in reading the meaning of bird flight, prophecies that Odysseus is near, and advises the suitors to drop their suit and leave. Eurymachus mocks Halitherses, denying his ability to prophecy and claiming that Odysseus is dead. He advises Telemachus to send Penelope home and have her father arrange a wedding for her. Telemachus responds with a request for a ship so that he can seek out news of Odysseus. If he's reported to be alive, Telemachus plans to wait a year; but if he hears of his father's death, he will give him a funeral and give his mother in marriage to another man.

Mentor then condemns the suitors and the Ithacans for the treatment of Odysseus' household, especially disgusting in the light of Odysseus' just reign as king over them. Leocritos says that if Odysseus comes home, the suitors will kill him.

Telemachus prays to Athena, and she appears to him as Mentor. "Mentor" encourages Telemachus to be like Odysseus and tells him to forget about the suitors for now: Mentor will procure a ship for Telemachus and sail with him. Mentor tells Telemachus that he should get provisions, and he goes home to do so. Antinous greets him, tells him that the Achaeans will provide a ship, and invites him to share a meal as he used to do. Telemachus refuses, saying he has no ship and that he knows that the suitors do not wish for him to have one. He promises that he will bring doom upon them if he can. In response, the suitors make fun of Telemachus and threaten him. Telemachus leaves them and gets the necessary stores from Eurycleia, swearing her to secrecy about his trip, and making her promise not to tell Penelope until at least the eleventh or twelfth day of his voyage, or when Penelope notices his absence. In the meantime, Athena, posing as Telemachus, borrows a ship from Noëmon and collects a crew. Telemachus, "Mentor," and the crew set sail in the swift ship, pouring out a libation to the gods.

# STRATEGY 8

## Setting—Real and Imaginary Places

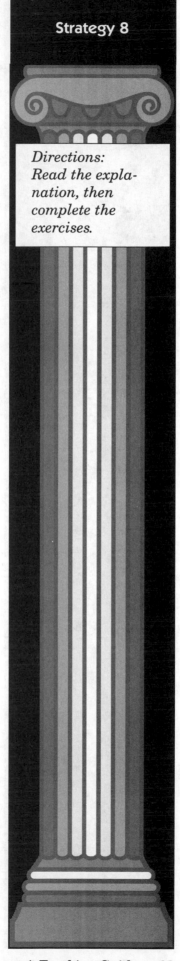

*Directions: Read the explanation, then complete the exercises.*

**Setting** is both the world in which the story takes place and the changing scenery that serves as the backdrop for each scene or chapter. Setting includes what the characters see, hear, smell, and can touch in their environment, including

- time of day
- season of the year
- plants and animals
- natural features

- weather
- landscape
- buildings or other structures

The general setting of this story is mainland Greece, the Peloponnese, the Greek islands to the west, and the waters around them in a time around a thousand years B.C., a region with certain kinds of people, certain kinds of landscape, certain plants and animals and weather, certain rules and customs. Because the wanderings of Odysseus are episodic, the setting changes for each adventure. After Odysseus arrives in Ithaca, however, in Book 13, the rest of the story takes place on this island.

Setting can serve different functions in different stories, and at different times in the same story. It may be a mere backdrop to the story, or it may play a more integral part. The setting may be symbolic and be a source of information about the inhabitants of the area. The setting may create conflicts for the characters of the story. The setting may help or hinder the characters in achieving their goals: it may provide materials or resources that help the characters solve problems, or create physical hardships or challenges that are difficult to overcome. Setting can also help establish characterization. Although an epic is mainly narrative, that is, a type of writing that tells a story, sections of an epic that deal with the setting are usually passages of description.

Homer uses a combination of real and imaginary settings. Sparta, Mycenae, Troy, Pylos—these are all real places, and can be located on our maps. But is what Homer called *Ithaca* the same Greek island that we call by that name today? Where is Olympus, home of the gods? Where can Scylla and Charybdis be found? Some of Homer's lands are real, but some are mythical. And with some, we can't be sure.

As you notice the setting, try to figure out what Homer is trying to convey. Pay attention to the possibilities and problems created by the setting, and the mood the setting creates for you in order to take advantage of any hints Homer is giving about what might happen next.

Extend the following chart to create a record of *Odyssey* settings.

| Page # | Setting Name | Setting Description |
|--------|--------------|--------------------|
|        |              |                    |
|        |              |                    |
|        |              |                    |

# Book 3

## Journal and Discussion Topics

1. What techniques does Homer use to indicate the passage of time?
2. How is the relationship between Athena and Poseidon portrayed?
3. What have you learned so far about the rules of hospitality in the society about which Homer writes?
4. What strategic mistake did Menelaus and Agamemnon make, according to Nestor?
5. Why, according to Nestor, should Telemachus hurry home?
6. How do people honor the gods in this society?
7. Why do you think there is such a detailed description of the sacrifices to Poseidon and Athena?

## Summary

Telemachus and "Mentor" (Athena in disguise) land at Pylos, the home of Nestor, as a sacrifice to Poseidon is being offered. They join in, at Nestor's request, and Athena/Mentor makes a prayer . . . and answers it herself. After dinner, Nestor questions his guests, and Telemachus asks for news of his father. Nestor, in response, recounts the losses of Ajax, Achilles, Patroclus, and Antilochus in Troy; remarks on Telemachus' similarity to Odysseus in looks and speech; and tells how the army split into 2 camps at the end of the war, Menelaus arguing that they should decamp immediately, and Agamemnon that they should offer a sacrifice first. Odysseus sided with Menelaus and Nestor and sailed from Troy with them, but turned back afterwards to rejoin Agamemnon. Nestor tells that he, himself, and his companions got home in fairly good time, and Menelaus wandered 7 years before reaching home. Nestor mentions Agamemnon's homecoming and murder, and then says he has heard of the suitors at Odysseus' house vying for Penelope. He refers to Athena's love for Odysseus, and gives his opinion that if Athena loved Telemachus as much, there would soon be an end to the trouble with the suitors.

Telemachus asks to hear the story of Agamemnon's homecoming, and Nestor tells it——how Aegisthus courted Clytemnestra; how after initially refusing him, she and he became lovers and planned the murder of Agamemnon; how 8 years after Agamemnon's death, Orestes killed Aegisthus and Clytemnestra. Nestor uses this story to warn Telemachus not to stay too long from home, but to call on Menelaus and return quickly. Nestor offers Telemachus horses to take him to Sparta and a place to sleep for the night. Athena/Mentor refuses a bed and departs in the form of a seahawk, revealing her identity to Nestor, who offers prayers to her. In the morning, Nestor offers sacrifice to Athena, and sends his own son Pisistratus to be a companion to Telemachus on his journey.

# Book 4

## Journal and Discussion Topics

1. What causes Menelaus to be angry with Eteoneus?
2. In your own words, explain the relationship between Menelaus and Odysseus.
3. List the deceptions you find in this book.
4. How does Menelaus explain Helen's role in trying to lure the Achaean fighters out of the wooden horse? Do you accept this explanation? Why or why not?
5. Draw a picture or a series of pictures showing the struggle between Menelaus and Proteus.
6. How does Telemachus refuse Menelaus' offer without offending him?
7. Why is Antinous angry with Telemachus? What does Antinous plan to do?
8. Why do you think Penelope weeps more for Telemachus than for Odysseus?
9. How does Athena answer Penelope's prayer?

## Summary

Pisistratus and Telemachus arrive in Sparta just in time to join in celebrating the double wedding of Menelaus' son and daughter. After the guests are fed, Menelaus begins reminiscing, and in mentioning his friends from his days in Troy, tells that the companion whom he misses most is Odysseus. Telemachus, hearing his father's name, begins to weep, and Helen and Menelaus recognize him as his father's son. Pisistratus confirms their surmise, and briefly describes the situation at Odysseus' home. Helen drugs the wine to allow a festive mood for the evening meal, and tells the story of how Odysseus entered Troy disguised as a beggar in order to spy. Then Menelaus tells the story of how Helen tried to trick the Greek fighters into coming out of the wooden horse by imitating the voices of their wives, and only Odysseus prevented Anticlus from calling out in answer and betraying them all.

In the morning, Menelaus asks why Telemachus has come to him, and Telemachus describes the situation at home. Menelaus expresses his disgust with the suitors' behavior, and answers Telemachus' request for news by telling that he wrestled with Proteus and was able to learn from him that Ajax and Agamemnon are dead, and that Odysseus is stranded on Calypso's island. Menelaus invites Telemachus to stay with him, but Telemachus refuses, saying he must return quickly to Ithaca.

Meanwhile, Antinous discovers from a question Noëmon asks that Telemachus has actually procured a ship and sailed to find news of his father. Antinous is furious and plans to intercept him and murder him before he reaches home. Medon, the crier, tells Penelope, and this is the first she hears of Telemachus' voyage. Antinous prepares a ship and moors her offshore, while Penelope prays to Athena, who sends a dream in the form of Penelope's sister, Iphthime, who reveals that Telemachus is accompanied by Athena, but refuses to tell any news of Odysseus.

## Essay Topics

1. The first 4 books of the *Odyssey* are often referred to as the Telemachy. How do they prepare the reader for the story of Odysseus?

2. Do you think Athena or Penelope is the most important woman in this story so far? Why?

3. Do you like Helen? Why or why not?

4. Do you see any change in Telemachus from Book 1 to Book 4? Explain.

5. What do you see as the themes or focus of the *Odyssey* so far?

6. What predictions do you have for the action of the rest of the book?

7. The father-son relationship is integral to this story. Think of another story in which the father-son relationship is important and explain why.

8. Pick another story in which a character seeks something on a journey. Compare the story you have chosen with Telemachus' search for his father.

9. Who is your favorite character so far? Why?

# Book 5

## Journal and Discussion Topics

1. How is Athena's speech to Zeus about Odysseus similar to what Mentor said in the assembly in Book 2? What do you make of this?
2. Why do you think Athena complains to Zeus a second time?
3. If you are reading Fitzgerald's translation, what distinguishes Hermes' speech?
4. To what motives does Calypso attribute Hermes' orders?
5. What deceptions do you find in this chapter?
6. Why do you think Odysseus would rather be with Penelope than Calypso? What gift is he willing to forego to pursue this goal?
7. Summarize Odysseus' fight to reach land in your own words.

## Summary

Athena returns to the council of the gods and again pleads Odysseus' case before Zeus. Zeus remarks that he thought she had the situation in hand, and then sends Hermes to speak to Calypso, ordering that Odysseus be allowed to leave on a raft, and (after traveling 20 days by sea) land on Scheria, the island of the Phaeacians, who will send him home. Hermes goes immediately to Calypso and delivers the message. Calypso accuses the gods of jealousy, but acknowledges that Zeus cannot be denied. Hermes leaves, and Calypso goes to find Odysseus where he sits weeping for his home and his wife. She presents the decision to let Odysseus go as her own, and promises not to use any tricks or spells against him.

Calypso gives Odysseus an ax and an auger, and he builds a raft. She gives him food, and causes a breeze to blow, and Odysseus sets sail. After 17 days, Poseidon, returning from Ethiopia, spots Odysseus, and blows up a storm. Odysseus is blown from the raft and almost drowns, when Leucothea finds him and advises him to swim for land and to tie her veil around him as a sash, which will prevent him from sinking. At first he thinks it safer to ignore her advice and cling to the remaining pieces of the raft. But after being hit again by a wave, he does as Leucothea advised. He drifts for 2 days and 2 nights, and is washed up against rocks, but Athena guides him to a landspit by a river, where he comes ashore. He kisses the ground, creeps under some bushes, and burrows into a pile of leaves to sleep.

Directions:
Read the explanation, then complete the exercises.

# STRATEGY 9     The Hero's Journey

Mythology expert, Joseph Campbell, in *The Hero with a Thousand Faces*, characterizes the hero's journey as having a set pattern on which a myriad of variations are played out. The hero leaves his ordinary life on a journey into a region where he confronts the supernatural. He wins a victory and returns to the world he left as a changed person. Not every stage is present in every story.

1. Read the summary of each stage in the hero's journey. Decide whether the stage seems to be present in the *Odyssey*. If you think it is, explain your ideas.

### DEPARTURE

I. **The Call to Adventure**
The hero can enter into the adventure by mistake, or by being called by a herald who summons the hero. The call comes at a time when the hero is ready for inner growth. The hero's focus shifts from home to a distant place.

II. **The Refusal of the Call**
The hero is not always eager to assume the adventure offered. The hero has the opportunity to reject the call. If the hero refuses, his or her life may enter a state of paralysis until something happens to release him or her.

III. **Supernatural Aid**
The hero encounters a helper as the journey begins: a guide and protector (often an old woman or an old man) who provides special powers to keep the hero safe in his or her encounters with evil. This protector usually appears to one who has already accepted the call, but not always. In fairy tales, the helper is often a wizard, hermit, smith, or shepherd.

IV. **The Crossing of the First Threshold**
The hero, accompanied by the guide, goes beyond the boundaries of his or her everyday life, enters the wilderness, and has a first encounter with the dangerous forces of the unknown.

V. **The Belly of the Whale**
The hero is swallowed up by the unknown.

### INITIATION

VI. **The Road of Trials**
The hero undergoes a series of trials, often on a perilous journey. The guide or other helpers support him. Each trial may bring new insight. Victories may be repeated, but are not lasting.

### RETURN

VII. **The Magic Flight**
The hero returns to the world from which s/he came, accompanied by his or her guardian.

VIII. **The Crossing of the Return Threshold**
The hero leaves the realm of the unknown and returns from the dark to the light. The transition is not easy.

IX. **Master of the Two Worlds**
The hero, through the journey, has won the ability to pass back and forth from one world to the other.

X. **Freedom to Live**
The hero can now live with new freedom as a result of the journey, having matured and grown.

# Writer's Forum                    Persuasion

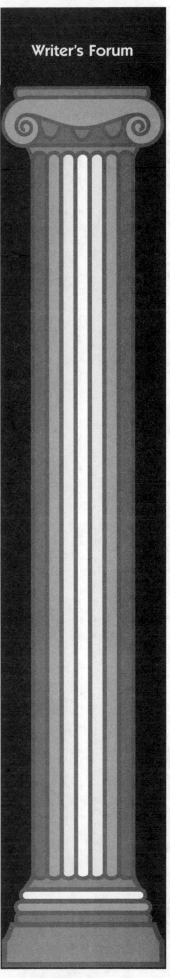

Persuasive discourse attempts to change what the audience thinks, believes, or values, or to move the audience to take action. In most persuasive discourse, the writer or speaker states a position and then provides evidence or reasons that attempt to convince the audience to embrace that position. Look back at Hermes' speech to Calypso. This is an example of persuasion.

Writers use a variety of techniques to make their writing persuasive. Some of these techniques are logical and reasonable and accepted in our culture as examples of convincing argument. Other techniques that appeal to the audience's prejudices or to instincts that most people would consider base (like greed) may be used by writers, but are often seen as inappropriate. Appeals to the audience's emotions are considered acceptable in some cases but not in others, and must be used carefully. Here are some examples of valid techniques for persuasion:

- Follow the standards for discourse in your community—make sure that your approach is courteous and presented in an appropriate forum. Hermes does not begin to speak until after he has finished his nectar and ambrosia. To do so would have been a breach of manners and jeopardized his mission.
- Tell the truth. If you cannot find convincing evidence, consider changing your point of view. Hermes can honestly say to Calypso that he is going to tell her nothing but the truth. His comments about how unappealing the trip is from Olympus show that he has no personal agenda.
- Appealing to authority is a way to substantiate your claims. Make sure that the authority you cite is well respected. When Hermes tells Calypso that Zeus is the source of the message he brings, he is appealing to authority.
- Use statistics and other numerical data. Hermes mentions the length of the Trojan War.
- Use other kinds of facts (not numerical) that are persuasive. Hermes tells Calypso that it is not possible to elude the will of Zeus. This is a fact in the world of the story.
- Make sure numerical and other facts are verified. You have a responsibility to present accurate information.
- Make your point in several different ways. This will help ensure that you have communicated clearly. Some ways of putting things will appeal to some people, and other ways will appeal to others. In the Lattimore translation, for example, Hermes ends by restating his goal in three different ways (Book 5, lines 112–115):

  1. "Now Zeus tells you to send him on his way with all speed."
  2. "It is not appointed for him to die here, away from his people."
  3. "It is still his fate that he shall see his people and come back to his house with the high roof and to the land of his fathers."

Organization can be important in persuasion. Think carefully about the order in which you will present your evidence or arguments. Writers are often urged to put the most important reason first (or last), and then organize the other reasons in descending (or ascending) order of importance.

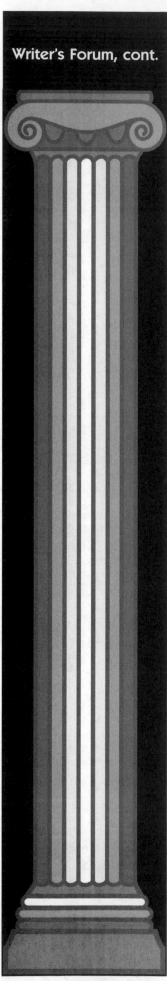

Knowing your audience is particularly important in persuasion. You need to know how their views differ from yours in order to know what points about your position to address. You need to anticipate their counterarguments in order to forestall them by showing why they either don't apply or are not valid. Hermes does this when he explains that he never would have come to Calypso's island of his own free will (even though he found the island delightful).

1. Choose a character in the *Odyssey* who wants something very much. Suggestions for your choice include Antinous, Odysseus, Telemachus, Penelope, Poseidon. Think about what audience the character you chose would need to address to get what s/he wanted. Write a persuasive monologue for your character. Use techniques from among those listed above.

# Book 6

## Journal and Discussion Topics

1. Why does Athena appear to Nausicaa in a dream?
2. How was doing laundry different for Nausicaa than it is for you?
3. Why do you think all the girls except for Nausicaa run away from Odysseus?
4. What techniques does Odysseus use in his speech to Nausicaa to please her?
5. Why does Nausicaa admonish her maids to return to her?
6. What purpose(s) do you think Nausicaa has in imagining for Odysseus what people might say about her?
7. Why doesn't Athena show herself to Odysseus?

## Summary

While Odysseus sleeps on Scheria, the island home of the Phaeacians, Athena appears in a dream to Nausicaa, the daughter of the islands' rulers, Alcinous and Arete. Taking the form of one of Nausicaa's friends, Athena reminds Nausicaa that she needs to go to the river to do laundry in preparation for her (not yet established) wedding. On arising, Nausicaa secures Alcinous' permission and sets off on the trip to the river with her maids. After they finish their laundry, Athena makes them stay and play until Odysseus awakens. Shielding his nakedness with a branch of the olive tree, Odysseus ventures out, and all the girls except Nausicaa run away. He praises her, tells her briefly of his plight, and asks her guidance to the town. She calls back her maids, chiding them for rudeness to a stranger, who, as such, is within Zeus' special providence. The maids give him clothes and oil for anointing himself, and he goes to bathe. Nausicaa directs Odysseus to follow the wagon back toward the palace, but to stop and wait in her father's garden so that she and her maids have a chance to reach the palace first. Then he should come out and ask directions to Alcinous' palace. Nausicaa suggests that Odysseus go straight to Arete and kneel in supplication before her. Odysseus does as Nausicaa bid him, pausing in the garden to invoke Athena and pray that he will be well treated by the Phaeacians. Athena hears him, but out of respect for Poseidon does not appear to him in her true form—that she reserves until he reaches Ithaca.

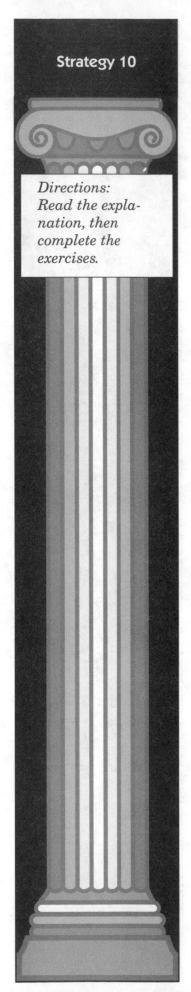

*Directions: Read the explanation, then complete the exercises.*

# STRATEGY 10   Similes and Metaphors

**Similes** and **metaphors** are figures of speech that compare two things that may be quite different in order to point out a similarity that is intended to give you a new perspective. These two methods of description get the reader's attention because they say something that may at first seem odd, surprising, unclear, or even inaccurate, and they draw the reader into the story by inviting the reader to figure out the point of the comparison.

Similes are usually signaled by the words *like, as, as when, so,* or *as if.* An example of a simile is "The voice of Zeus is like thunder." A metaphor, on the other hand, is a comparison in which it is stated that one thing **is** another. An example of a metaphor is, "Athena's wrath is fire." If the verb *to be* is not used, then you have an **implied metaphor.** A simile that goes on for a while, showing more than one point of comparison, is called an **extended simile.** Look at these translations of passages from the *Odyssey:*

A.  Fawns in a lion's lair!  As if a doe
    put down her litter of sucklings there, while she
    quested a glen or cropped some grassy hollow.
    Ha!  Then the lord returns to his own bed
    and deals out wretched doom on both alike.
    So will Odysseus deal out doom on these. ~Fitzgerald, page 63

B.  As when a doe has brought her fawns to the lair of a lion
    and put them there to sleep, they are newborn and still suckling,
    then wanders out into the foothills and the grassy corners,
    grazing there, but now the lion comes back to his own lair
    and visits a shameful destruction on both mother and children;
    so Odysseus will visit shameful destruction on these men.
    ~Lattimore, pages 73–74

C.  So there was Odysseus lying under the leaves, like a smouldering
    brand which some one has buried under black ashes far away in the
    country, with no one living near: that is how he keeps the seed of fire,
    or else he would have to go elsewhere for a light.  ~Rouse, page 72

D.  As a man will bury his glowing brand in black ashes,
    off on a lonely farmstead, no neighbors near,
    to keep a spark alive—no need to kindle fire
    from somewhere else—so great Odysseus buried
    himself in leaves. . . .  ~Fagles, page 167

1.  Identify the figures of speech used in each translation.

2.  What meaning do you get from the figurative language in each case?

3.  Compare and contrast the two renderings of each passage.

4.  Find the extended simile in Book 6, and tell what it means to you.

# Book 7

## Journal and Discussion Topics

1. Why is Arete so greatly honored?
2. What details indicate the wealth of Arete's and Alcinous' palace?
3. What plans for his newly arrived guest does Alcinous express in his first speech?
4. How does Odysseus turn aside Alcinous' anger with Nausicaa?
5. What signs does Alcinous give that he is impressed with Odysseus?

## Summary

After Nausicaa reaches home, Odysseus sets out from the garden, hidden in a fog created by Athena. Athena appears to him in the form of a child and guides him to Alcinous' palace, urging him to appeal to Arete, whose history she briefly recounts to him. Odysseus' quest for Arete leads him to see the beauties of the palace, while he is still being protected from sight by the cloud of fog. When he finds Arete, just as the Phaeacians are about to retire for the night, he grasps her knees in supplication and begs for passage to his home. Then he retires to sit among the ashes by the fire. Echeneus, the oldest Phaeacian, chides Alcinous for leaving his guest in the ashes, and Alcinous seats Odysseus beside him, ordering water for him to cleanse his hands and food and drink for him. Alcinous orders that the following day be a feast day in their guest's honor and declares that the Phaeacians will see that he gets home. Alcinous warns his people that their guest may be a god in disguise, but Odysseus assures them that he is mortal.

Everyone retires to bed except the 2 rulers and their guest, and after Odysseus is done with his meal, Arete asks him who he is and where he got Phaeacian clothing. While choosing not to reveal his name, Odysseus tells briefly of being shipwrecked, losing all his companions, being detained by Calypso, his release from her island, his treacherous trip that landed him on Scheria, and his meeting with Nausicaa. Alcinous finds fault with Nausicaa for not bringing Odysseus with her, but Odysseus defends her, saying (falsely) that she told him to follow the maids but he would not for fear of offending Alcinous. Alcinous answers by offering Odysseus a home in his land and Nausicaa as his bride, or passage to his own home on the following day. Odysseus pleads to be returned home, and all 3 retire to bed.

# STRATEGY 11     Characterization

A **character** in a story is someone or something whose actions, choices, thoughts, ideas, words, and influence are important in developing the plot of the story. Characters are often people, but also include other living creatures, gods, and sometimes even nonliving things. A force, such as good or evil, can operate as a character in a story.

Most stories have a single character or a small group of characters whose goal or problem is the core of the plot. This character or group of characters is called the **protagonist**. The protagonist does not have to be good, but a good protagonist may be referred to as the "hero" of the story. Readers usually identify with the protagonist and hope that the protagonist will succeed in attaining his or her goal. The character, group, or force that opposes the protagonist is called the **antagonist**. In certain stories, this character may be referred to as the "villain."

Characters, whether human or not, have what we call "personality"—a set of traits and features by which we recognize them. Personality is what helps us distinguish one suitor from another suitor, for example, whereas otherwise we might confuse them. **Characterization** is the name for the techniques a writer uses to reveal the personality of characters to the reader. Characterization is achieved in a number of different ways:

- **WORDS**—comments by the narrator, dialogue by others about the character, as well as the character's own words; what is said, as well as *how* it is said: dialect, slang, and tone are important
- **THOUGHTS**—what is going on in the character's mind, and the character's motives and choices
- **APPEARANCE**—the character's physical characteristics and clothing
- **ACTIONS**—what the character does
- **INTERACTIONS**—how the character relates to others
- **NAMES**—often symbolic of a major character trait or role
- **CHOSEN SETTING**—the items, furnishings, etc., that the character chooses to surround him- or herself with
- **CHANGE/DEVELOPMENT**—the occurrence of and direction of change or development a character undergoes inwardly

1. What techniques does Homer use to characterize Arete?

2. How much does Homer use thoughts as a characterization technique? Why do you think he does this?

3. How does Odysseus interact with others?

4. Critic Erich Auerbach claims that Homeric heroes like Achilles and Odysseus "have no development" (*Mimesis,* "Odysseus' Scar," page 17). As you continue reading, decide whether or not you agree with Auerbach. Write your conclusions here.

5. How would you characterize Athena and her role in the story so far?

# Book 8

## Journal and Discussion Topics

1. What deceptions occur in this book?
2. What do you make of the young athletes names?
3. What points does Odysseus make in his reply to the challenges to join the contest?
4. How does Alcinous show in actions his ideas about what being a host means?
5. How would you describe the view of the gods presented in this book?
6. What is special about the Phaeacian ships?
7. Why do you think Odysseus asks Demodocus for the song?
8. What reasons does Alcinous give for Odysseus to reveal himself?
9. If you were Odysseus, would you feel that the gifts of Seareach/Broadsea/ Euryalos made up for his rudeness?

## Summary

While Alcinous and Odysseus rest by the assembly ground, Athena disguises herself as the king's crier, arranges Odysseus' voyage home, and prepares Odysseus to win the day's contests. Alcinous then gives his own orders for his people to make ready for Odysseus' journey (although he still doesn't know who his guest is), calls the minstrel to sing to them, and goes home to prepare the sacrifice. Demodocus chooses to sing about the argument between Odysseus and Achilles, and Odysseus weeps into his mantle. Seeing Odysseus' distress, Antinous announces a pentathlon competition. Alcinous' son, Laodamas, has the idea of inviting Odysseus to compete, but Odysseus declines. One of the Phaeacians (Seareach/Broadsea/Euryalos) suggests that Odysseus' refusal comes from a lack of skill. Angered, Odysseus rebukes him, picks up a discus, and sails it far beyond all the others. Athena, again in the guise of a Phaeacian, declares him the winner. Odysseus, still affronted, offers to compete with a bow or a spear, but Alcinous graciously smoothes over the disagreement and invites the Phaeacians to demonstrate a dance for Odysseus. Demodocus sings of Ares and Aphrodite being caught by Hephaestus in a golden net. In the tale, Poseidon promises to pay Ares' debt, and Hephaestus sets Ares and Aphrodite free, whereupon they both run away. Odysseus enjoys the story and praises the dancers. Then Alcinous and his princes bring gifts, and suggest that Seareach/Broadsea/ Euryalos use this opportunity to make up for his breach of good manners, which he does by presenting Odysseus with a beautiful broadsword and sheathe. Odysseus is given a bath, and as he passes by, Nausicaa asks him to remember her, which he promises to do. When they sit down to supper, he sends the best portion of his meat to Demodocus and asks him to sing of the Trojan horse. The minstrel obeys, and Odysseus weeps. Hearing him, Alcinous stops Demodocus, and suggests that the time has come for Odysseus to identify himself and tell his story. As Alcinous speaks, he reveals that Poseidon is not happy with the Phaeacians because their ships are so safe and secure, and there is a prediction that a ship will one day be destroyed by Poseidon.

**Essay Topics**

1. Do you identify more with Telemachus or Odysseus? Explain your response.

2. If you could visit either Nestor, Menelaus, or Alcinous, whom would you visit and why?

3. How do you think Odysseus will respond to Alcinous' request that he identify himself? Explain your reasoning. Why do you think he has kept his identity to himself so far?

4. Choose one element of the Greek culture presented in this story and contrast it with your culture. Analyze the causes for the differences you perceive.

5. Now that you have read part of the story that focuses on Odysseus, what is your judgment about Homer's choice to begin with the Telemachy? Identify the criteria that you have used in making your evaluation.

6. In your opinion, does the interchange between Seareach/Broadsea/Euryalos and Odysseus add anything to the section of the story on Scheria? If so, what? Explain why you think as you do.

7. What parallels do you find between the plot of Books 5–8 and that of Books 1–4?

8. All the arrangements for Odysseus' homecoming have been made by Alcinous and Athena. Do you think things will go smoothly on the voyage? Why or why not? What do you think will happen?

# Book 9

## Journal and Discussion Topics

1. What does Odysseus do that would lead you to judge that he is a good leader?
2. Which of Odysseus' judgments do you think were questionable? Explain why you think so and what factors you think influenced Odysseus' decisions.
3. What details show that the Cyclops are uncivilized?
4. What deceptions do you find in this book?
5. What part of this book is most vivid in your memory? Why?
6. How does the narration change in this book?

## Summary

The story switches to the first-person point of view narrated by Odysseus. [**Note:** We will use past tense for the material Odysseus narrates in Books 9–12.] After praising Demodocus' song, Odysseus begins by telling his name, identifying his homeland, and summarizing his accomplishments and journey by telling briefly of being detained by Calypso and Circe. He then returns to the departure from Troy.

First Odysseus and his men landed at the land of the Cicones, and (apparently without provocation) Odysseus and his men attacked the people and took plunder and slaves. But Odysseus' men refused to obey his order to return to the ships, so the army of the Cicones came upon them, and they lost many men fighting their way back to their ships. They encountered a storm, and having weathered that, they approached close to Ithaca, but a current took them back out to sea, and they ended up at the land of the Lotus Eaters. Landing to get water, they prepared a meal and Odysseus sent messengers to find out about the inhabitants. When they did not return, Odysseus sought them out and discovered that from eating the Lotus flower they had lost their desire to return home. He took them back to the ships by force, and then ordered everyone else aboard and set off.

They approached the land of the Cyclops, uncivilized giants without laws, agriculture, government, traditions, or shipbuilding (and therefore no foreign commerce), but Odysseus did not know that at the time. After a meal, Odysseus decided to find out what sort of inhabitants the land had. After seeing a huge man in a cave, Odysseus left most of the crew near the ship, and taking his 12 best fighters, a skin of strong liquor, and some food, he led the group to the cave. But the Cyclops had gone to the fields with his sheep. After looking around, the men suggested to Odysseus that they steal the cheeses and sheep and flee. But Odysseus refused, wishing to see what the man would offer them as gifts.

The Cyclops returned, and leaving the rams outside, brought the ewes into the cave to milk and placed an enormous rock in front of the door to block it. Only after he had finished with the ewes did he see Odysseus and his men, and he immediately asked them their identity and origins. Odysseus replied that they were warriors from Troy, blown off course and depending on his mercy as strangers protected by Zeus. The Cyclops informed them that he cared nothing

about Zeus, and asked for the location of their ship. Odysseus lied and said they were shipwrecked, at which news, the Cyclops grabbed 2 of the men and ate them. Odysseus grabbed his sword and prepared to kill the Cyclops in revenge, but stopped, realizing that if he did they would be trapped in the cave since only the Cyclops could move the great stone from the door. In the morning, the Cyclops ate another 2 of Odysseus' companions and left to pasture his flock, replacing the great stone behind him. While he was gone, Odysseus planned how to use a tree trunk left in the cave to put out the Cyclops' eye, and the companions drew lots to see who would help Odysseus carry out the plan.

When the Cyclops returned, he brought both ewes and rams into the cave and moved the rock into place. He ate 2 more men, and Odysseus offered him some of the special wine and chastised him for his lack of hospitality. In return, the Cyclops asked Odysseus' name and offered him a special gift. Odysseus said his name was "Nobody," and the Cyclops explained the gift was that "Nobody" will be the last man to be eaten and immediately fell into a drunken sleep. Odysseus heated the olive trunk in the fire and the men helped him to drive it into the Cyclops' eye. The Cyclops tried to grab the men and then began yelling for the other Cyclops. They asked if he was okay, and he replied that "Nobody" had tricked him. The other Cyclops thought it was a joke and went away.

Plotting an escape, Odysseus roped sets of 3 rams together and tied a companion under the middle of each set. He himself hung under the biggest, woolliest ram, and when morning came and the Cyclops opened the door, the men escaped under the rams.

Taking the flocks with them onto the ship, they set out to sea. But Odysseus called out to let Polyphemus know that he'd been tricked. In response, the Cyclops threw a hilltop at the ship and almost sank it. Over the crew's protest, Odysseus again called to Polyphemus, telling him that he was really Odysseus from Ithaca. Polyphemus realized that Odysseus' coming had been foretold, but he had expected a giant, not a puny man. He prayed to his father, Poseidon, that Odysseus would never reach his home or that if he did, it would not be for a long time and all his crew would die, and Poseidon heard him. After sharing the flocks with the crews of the other ships, the group made an offering, but Zeus refused it. The next morning, Odysseus prepared to set sail again, and the men mourned the loss of the friends the Cyclops had eaten.

# STRATEGY 12

## Cross-Cultural Parallels—Fin MacCumhail

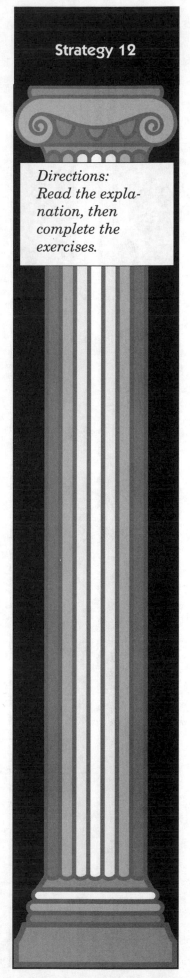

*Directions: Read the explanation, then complete the exercises.*

Some stories with amazingly similar plots can be found in cultures from very different parts of the world. An episode in the adventures of the Irish hero, Fin MacCumhail (pronounced fin mac-cool), has many similar elements to the story of Odysseus and Polyphemus. Read this excerpted version of Fin's adventure from *Myths and Folklore of Ireland,* by Jeremiah Curtin, pages 210–211.

"Fin and Bran [his dog] went on till they came to a great cave, in which they found a herd of goats. At the further end of the cave was a smouldering fire. The two lay down to rest.

"A couple of hours later, in came a giant with a salmon in his hand. This giant was of awful height, he had but one eye, and that in the middle of his forehead, as large as the sun in heaven.

"When he saw Fin, he called out: 'Here, take this salmon and roast it; but be careful, for if you raise a single blister on it I'll cut the head off you. . . .'

"The giant lay down to sleep in the middle of the cave. Fin spitted the salmon, and held it over the fire.

"The minute the giant closed the one eye in his head, he began to snore. Every time he drew breath into his body, he dragged Fin, the spit, the salmon, Bran, and all the goats to his mouth; and every time he drove a breath out of himself, he threw them back to the places they were in before. Fin was drawn time after time to the mouth of the giant with such force, that he was in dread of going down his throat.

"When partly cooked, a blister rose on the salmon. Fin pressed the place with his thumb, to know could he break the blister, and hide from the giant the harm that was done. But he burned his thumb, and, to ease the pain, put it between his teeth and gnawed the skin to the flesh, the flesh to the bone, and the bone to the marrow; and when he had tasted the marrow, he received the knowledge of all things. Next moment, he was drawn by the breath of the giant right up to his face, and, knowing from his thumb what to do, he plunged the hot spit into the sleeping eye of the giant and destroyed it.

"That instant the giant with a single bound was at the low entrance of the cave, and, standing with his back to the wall and a foot on each side of the opening, roared out: 'You'll not leave this place alive.'

"Now Fin killed the largest goat, skinned him as quickly as he could, then putting the skin on himself he drove the herd to where the giant stood; the goats passed out one by one between his legs. When the great goat came the giant took him by the horns. Fin slipped from the skin, and ran out."

1. Identify the similarities between this story and the story of the escape from the Cyclops in Book 9 of the *Odyssey*.

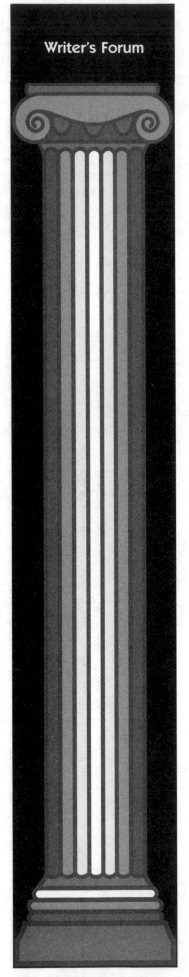

# Writer's Forum

## Comparison and Contrast

**Comparing** and **contrasting** puts 2 or more subjects side by side in order to draw insights from their similarities and differences.

In a compare and contrast essay, you show the similarities and differences between 2 people, things, ideas, approaches, etc., and draw some conclusion based on this examination. You choose the categories to compare and contrast based on your purpose, and these categories will change depending on your topic. For example, if you were comparing and contrasting Athena and Poseidon, you might choose categories such as "role in story," "relationship with Odysseus," "knowledge," and "appearance." If, however, you were contrasting the setting of Scheria with the setting of the Cyclops' land, you would use different categories. A Venn diagram or a chart can help you organize the information you will use. A Venn diagram shows visually what two or more subjects have in common and what characteristics they have that they do not share.

Here is an example:

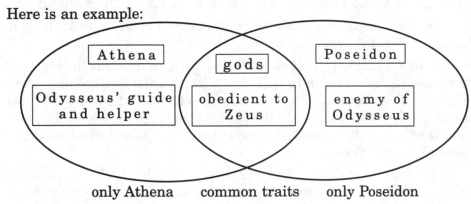

| only Athena | common traits | only Poseidon |

Source words that can help you express concepts of similarity and difference include the following:

SIMILARITY

- as well as
- similarly
- likewise
- alike
- at the same time
- resemble

DIFFERENCE

- differ
- whereas
- however
- while
- but
- on the contrary
- conversely
- though
- on the other hand

There are 2 standard ways to organize a compare and contrast essay. One possibility is to give all the information about one of the items being compared and contrasted first. Then, as you go through the information for the second item, you can point out which characteristics are held in common and which are unique. Another approach is to go through each characteristic, one at a time, and tell the information about that one characteristic for each item being compared/contrasted before moving on to the next characteristic.

It's usually a good idea to choose your organizational method before you begin writing.

1. Write an essay comparing and contrasting the episode about Fin MacCumhail with the story of Odysseus' visit to Polyphemus.

# Book 10

## Journal and Discussion Topics

1. What causes the change in Aeolus' attitude toward Odysseus?
2. What is unusual about the land of the Laestrygonians?
3. Compare and contrast the Cyclops and the Laestrygonians.
4. Characterize the style of Hermes' speech in Fitzgerald's translation, pages 173–174. (If you are using a different translation, go to 5.)
5. How does Circe recognize Odysseus?
6. What transformations occur in this chapter?
7. What makes Odysseus think of killing Eurylochus?
8. Why are the Achaeans distressed even though Circe is helping them depart?

## Summary

Odysseus and his crew landed at the island kingdom of Aeolus, king of the winds, who entertained them for a month. Upon their departure, Aeolus gave Odysseus a bag containing winds to help them on their way. They sailed for 9 days till they were so close to Ithaca that they could see people building fires on the beach, and having worked the sails for 9 days by himself, Odysseus fell asleep. The crew, suspecting that the bag from Aeolus was full of treasure that Odysseus was keeping for himself, untied the bag and unleashed all the winds at once, creating an enormous storm that blew them back to Aeolus' land. Odysseus waited by the door of the dining hall and asked Aeolus to help them again, but Aeolus said that their voyage was cursed by the gods, and sent them away.

They next landed in the country of the Laestrygonians and moored their ships, though Odysseus moored his separately from the rest. Going up a path, Odysseus' 3 messengers found first the daughter, then the wife, of the king, Antiphates, a man-eating giant who immediately ate one of the men. The other 2 messengers raced back to the ships, followed by the king and the other Laestrygonians, who stoned the ships and killed the men, and only the crew of Odysseus' own ship escaped.

Next they arrived at the island of Circe. After several days of mourning, Odysseus went a little away to look around and found a stag, which he shot to feed his crew. After they had eaten, he divided the crew into 2 groups. One, he led himself; the other was led by Eurylochus. Eurylochus' group came upon the dwelling of Circe, who sat at her loom, singing. All the crew cried out to her, entered her house, and ate her food, which turned them into swine—all except Eurylochus, who had feared a trap and stayed outside. When Circe had consigned the men to a pigsty, Eurylochus ran back to the ship and told Odysseus what he had seen. He refused to lead Odysseus back to Circe's house, so Odysseus set off alone, but met Hermes on the way. Hermes told him how to avoid enchantment and free his men from Circe's spell, and gave him an herb called *moly* to protect him. Odysseus followed Hermes' directions, and from the fact that he was not enchanted, Circe divined that he was Odysseus, whose coming had been foretold to her by Hermes. She released his men from enchantment,

but told him to have his remaining crew members pull the ship ashore and join the group already with her.

The other men prepared to follow Odysseus, but Eurylochus resisted, recalling to the group that Odysseus' poor judgment had led to the death of the men at Polyphemus' hands. Odysseus was so angry he thought of killing Eurylochus, but he didn't. They set out for Circe's, and when they arrived, found their mates bathed and clothed by Circe, who invited them to stay until their bodies and spirits were restored. After many months had passed, Odysseus' crew finally called to his mind their desire to return to Ithaca. Odysseus requested Circe's help, and she agreed that they might leave, but she told Odysseus that they needed to travel home by way of the Land of the Dead so that he could speak to Tiresias, a shade. Odysseus was distraught, but Circe gave him careful instructions about making a sacrifice when he reached the Land of the Dead, so that Tiresias could speak and give him instructions on how to return home.

Odysseus roused his men and bid them prepare to sail. But the youngest of the crew, Elpenor, had fallen asleep on the roof of the house, and when he heard the calls of the others and arose to follow them, he missed his footing and fell to his death. It seems that Odysseus wasn't immediately aware of his death. He was busy telling the rest of the crew that they must go by the Land of the Dead, and the crew was nearly hysterical. Arriving at the ship, they found that Circe had provided the animals needed for the sacrifice they would have to make.

# Book 11

Book 11

## Journal and Discussion Topics

1. What promises are made in this book?
2. What warnings does Tiresias give Odysseus?
3. How does Agamemnon contradict himself?
4. What is your opinion about responsibility for the situation between Clytemnestra and Agamemnon?
5. What is the effect on the Phaeacians of Odysseus' tale of visiting with the dead?
6. Which shade interests you most? Why?
7. What is it like to be dead, according to these portrayals?
8. Find all the mentions of sons in Book 11. What do you think they point to?

## Summary

Odysseus and his men set sail from Circe's island, following her directions for finding Tiresias in the Land of the Dead. As Circe directed, Odysseus dug a pit and prepared the sacrifices, and the souls began to appear. Odysseus spoke first to Elpenor, who, after revealing how he came to die, prayed that Odysseus would return to Circe's island to bury and mourn him before going home. Odysseus promised to fulfill the request. Next came Odysseus' mother, Anticleia, but Odysseus held her off, waiting for Tiresias.

Tiresias came and warned Odysseus of a difficult time to come, due to the wrath of Poseidon. He warned Odysseus that only self-denial, restraint of his crew, and avoidance of Helios' cattle would insure his safety. Barring this, Odysseus would be the sole survivor. He would return home only to find trouble in his house, and though he would be able to kill the suitors one way or another, he would have to go on a trip on foot, carrying an oar, till he came to a land where people would mistake the oar for a winnowing fan. There he would have to sacrifice to Poseidon. In the end, he would die at sea at a good old age.

Speaking to his mother, Odysseus found out that Penelope had not remarried but remained with Telemachus, who had become a magistrate; that Laertes was living in poverty, longing for his son's return; and that Anticleia had died of longing for her son. Odysseus tried to embrace her, but could not.

Then Odysseus spoke to Tyro, Antiope, Alcmena, Megara, Epicaste (Jocasta), Chloris, Leda, Iphimedeia, Phaedra, Procris, Ariadne, Maera, Clymene, Eriphyle, and many others.

After relating this part of his story, Odysseus falls silent, and it is Arete who speaks, asking her people how they view Odysseus now, and encouraging them to be generous to him. Echeneus, the oldest citizen, agrees and defers to Alcinous, who suggests that Odysseus delay his voyage one day so that they can bestow more gifts on him. Odysseus agrees, saying he would even stay a year in order that he might return home with wealth, because that would bring him greater honor when he reaches home. Alcinous then praises Odysseus' storytelling ability and asks Odysseus whether he met any of his companions from Troy in the Land of the Dead and, if so, to tell about these encounters. Odysseus replies that after the women were gone, Agamemnon was the first

man to appear. Odysseus asked Agamemnon how he died, and Agamemnon told how Aegisthus and Clytemnestra killed him and how even when he was dying, he tried to save Cassandra by grabbing the sword blade as Clytemnestra attacked her. Agamemnon first told Odysseus that Odysseus had nothing to fear from Penelope because she is wise, but then he said that no wives are faithful anymore and he should return home secretly with no warning. Then Agamemnon asked for news of Orestes, but Odysseus could not give him any.

Next came Achilles, Patroclus, Antilochus, Ajax, and Achilles, who asked Odysseus how he came there. Odysseus explained that he needed Tiresias' prophetic vision. Explaining that he had not yet reached home and consequently leads a life of pain, Odysseus asked Achilles why he was so dissatisfied among the dead. Achilles said that it is better to be the poorest slave among men than to be lord of all the dead. Then he, too, asked for news of a son, Neoptolemus, and also of his father, Peleus. Odysseus didn't know anything about Peleus, but he told Achilles how he went to bring Neoptolemus from Skyros to Troy, where he became the finest speaker barring only Nestor and Odysseus and fought like a champion. Neoptolemus was the only man who was not nervous when Odysseus prepared to lead the group out of their hiding place in the Trojan horse, and he came through that episode without even a scratch. Hearing this, Achilles left, happy for his son's success.

Next came Telamonian Ajax, still angry because Odysseus, rather than he, received Achilles' arms after Achilles died. Odysseus called to him, trying to make peace, but Ajax wouldn't even answer him. Odysseus then briefly glimpsed Minos, Orion, Tityos, Tantalus, Sisyphus, and Heracles (Hercules) who spoke to Odysseus. Odysseus wanted to stay to see Theseus and Pirithous, but a crowd of shades gathered and Odysseus was afraid and ran with his crew for the ship.

# STRATEGY 13      Plot Elements

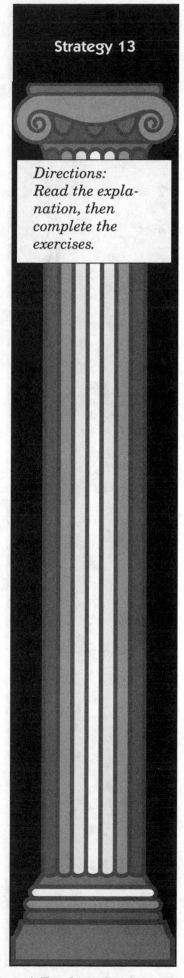

*Directions: Read the explanation, then complete the exercises.*

Recall the beginning of the Telemachy (Book 1) and the beginning of Book 5. Both begin with Athena interceding for Odysseus with Zeus and a divine messenger being dispatched to earth. Based on this and other similarities, we can say that these 2 sections of the *Odyssey* have similar plots. Vladimir Propp, a Russian folklorist (b. 1895), spent many years analyzing plot elements. His famous book on the structure of folktales is called *Morphology of the Folktale*. Although the study that produced that work was limited to a certain kind of fairy tale, recent scholarship has suggested that his categories can be applied to other folktales and even to epic, dances, games, novels, and comic strips (Introduction, page xiv). Here, in brief form, are Propp's categories:

    I. One of the members of a family absents himself from home.
    II. An interdiction [warning] is addressed to the hero.
    III. The interdiction is violated.
    IV. The villain makes an attempt at reconnaissance [researching his victim].
    V. The villain receives information about his victim.
    VI. The villain attempts to deceive his victim in order to take possession of him or of his belongings.
    VII. The victim submits to deception and thereby unwittingly helps his enemy.
    VIII. The villain causes harm or injury to a member of the family.
    VIIIa. One member of the family either lacks or desires to have something.
    IX. Misfortune or lack is made known; the hero is approached with a request or command; he is allowed to go or he is dispatched.
    X. The seeker agrees to or decides upon counteraction.
    XI. The hero leaves home.
    XII. The hero is tested, interrogated, attacked, etc., which prepares the way for his receiving either a magical agent or helper [donor].
    XIII. The hero reacts to the actions of the future donor.
    XIV. The hero acquires the use of a magical agent.
    XV. The hero is transferred, delivered, or led to the whereabouts of an object of search.
    XVI. The hero and the villain join in direct combat.
    XVII. The hero is branded.
    XVIII. The villain is defeated.
    XIX. The initial misfortune or lack is liquidated [ended].
    XX. The hero returns.
    XXI. The hero is pursued.
    XXII. Rescue of the hero from pursuit.
    XXIII. The hero, unrecognized, arrives home or in another country.
    XXIV. A false hero presents unfounded claims.
    XXV. A difficult task is proposed to the hero.
    XXVI. The task is resolved [completed by the hero].
    XXVII. The hero is recognized.
    XXVIII. The false hero or villain is exposed.
    XXIX. The hero is given a new appearance.
    XXX. The villain is punished.
    XXXI. The hero is married and ascends the throne.

1. Review the elements from I to XXIII. Identify as many elements as you can that you believe are included in the Telemachy. Explain how each element fits in.

2. In the introduction to the second edition of *Morphology of the Folktale*, Alan Dundes writes, "it is noteworthy that the last portion of the *Odyssey* is strikingly similar to Propp's functions 23–31." When you have finished reading the *Odyssey*, write a defense of Dundes's claim, using evidence from the story to support your assertions.

# Book 12

## Journal and Discussion Topics

1. About what does Circe give Odysseus advice? What does she leave to his discretion?
2. Where in the *Odyssey* did you first hear about Helios' cattle?
3. Compare and contrast the warnings of Circe and Tiresias about Helios' cattle.
4. What do the Sirens offer? Why is it tempting?
5. What does Circe tell Odysseus that he doesn't tell his crew? Why does he choose not to tell? Do you feel that he is justified? Explain.
6. Explain the simile comparing Scylla and the fisherman.
7. Read Exodus chapter 32 from the Old Testament. Compare and contrast this story with the incident on Helios' island.
8. In your own words, retell Odysseus' return through Scylla and Charybdis.

## Summary

Odysseus and his crew returned to Circe's island in order to fulfill his promise to Elpenor. They built a funeral pyre, mourned him as he burned, and then made him a barrow. Circe came with her maids, bringing the crew a meal, and telling them they could relax until the following morning, when they would again set sail with her guidance for their voyage. The crew enjoyed themselves, and when they had all fallen asleep, Circe led Odysseus away to give him private counsel.

First, she warned him about the Sirens, beautiful women who sing to passing ships and lure sailors to their island, enchanting them so that they never return home. Circe warned Odysseus to plug his men's ears with beeswax, but told him that if he wanted to hear the Siren's song, he could safely do so by having the men tie him to the mast and warning them not to untie him until the Sirens are safely passed.

Next, she said, he would encounter the wandering rocks, called Drifters, that only one ship—the *Argo*—had ever passed safely. She described an alternative course, between headlands. On one side, there is a cave in a sheer cliff where Scylla, a 12-legged, 6-headed monster lives. She takes 6 men from each ship that passes, one man to feed each of her 6 heads. On the opposite side, under a hanging fig tree, is the whirlpool Charybdis, which can suck a whole ship under. Circe advised that it is better to lose 6 men than to lose all. Odysseus asked if there was a way to fight off Scylla, but Circe said the best hope is for the men to row with all their might and escape a second strike from her.

In a speech in which several lines are exactly the same as in Tiresias' warning, Circe warned Odysseus to avoid Helios' cattle, lest he lose all his shipmates and spend many more years at sea before his homecoming. At dawn, Circe left him, and Odysseus roused his men, and when they had the ship under way, he spoke to them, saying that it was important for all to know what Circe foretold, but only sharing with them her comments about the Sirens. Odysseus personally put the wax in the crew's ears. Then, the sailors tied him up, and he listened to the Siren's song as they told him that they know everything about Troy and the world. Once the ship had passed out of range, the crew removed the wax and untied Odysseus.

Immediately, the ship came into swift water. Odysseus gave the crew orders to row hard, and particularly warned the man at the tiller to keep them toward the headland (following Circe's advice) or they would all drown, but without revealing the dangers of Scylla and Charybdis. As they passed, Scylla—as predicted—grabbed 6 men, and Odysseus tells the Phaeacians that the worst sight he ever saw at sea was Scylla eating his men.

Leaving Scylla and Charybdis behind brought them to Helios' island, and Odysseus recalling the warnings, sadly told the crew that they could not land on the island where they could hear the cattle lowing. Eurylochus led the protest of the crew, demanding that they go ashore. Being one against the rest, Odysseus submitted, but only after having the men swear an oath that they would not harm any cattle, but would eat only the food Circe gave them. After they landed the ship, he reminded them again not to touch the cattle. But they ended up unable to leave the island because of the winds, and their food ran out. Odysseus went inland to pray to the gods in solitude, and fell asleep. While he was gone, Eurylochus rallied the crew and persuaded them to sacrifice and eat some of Helios' cattle, promising that they would build a temple to Helios when they got home. He said he preferred death from Helios' wrath to starving to death. Odysseus awoke suddenly and returned to the coast, and as soon as he smelled the cooking, cried out to Zeus and the gods, and (as Odysseus found out later from Calypso) Helios did too, asking that Zeus punish Odysseus' men, and threatening to leave the sky and light the underworld instead if Zeus would not act. Zeus soothed Helios, saying that he would split the ship with a lightning bolt.

On the seventh day, they set sail in fair weather, but a storm struck and Zeus did hit the ship with lightning, killing all hands but Odysseus, who managed to tie the mast and keel together and straddle them to try to ride out the storm. Driven back north between Scylla and Charybdis, but this time on Charybdis' side, Odysseus' raft got sucked into the whirlpool, and he leapt from it to grab onto the fig tree that overhangs Charybdis. There he hung until the whirlpool spit his raft up again, dropped from the fig tree to land on his raft, and paddled with his hands to get past Scylla. After 9 days at sea, he landed on Calypso's island, and that being the point at which he started speaking to the Phaeacians, Odysseus chooses to stop, rather than repeat himself and be considered a boring storyteller.

# STRATEGY 14 Theme

*Directions:
Read the expla-
nation, then
complete the
exercises.*

The **theme** of a story might be thought of as the story's point or its message. A theme is usually a generalization about life or human behavior or values, true, but not a truism—the author's insight into the way things are that s/he wants to share with readers. Theme is an important part of a story's meaning and is developed throughout the story. And it is important to note that a story can have multiple themes and meanings.

A persuasive or didactic piece of writing (such as a fable) might have an explicit moral—a clear statement of theme. Such a statement can clearly convey the author's idea of what the story means, while limiting interpretation of the piece on the part of the reader. However, a piece of writing that was written with experience or aesthetic response in mind is more open to interpretation. Certainly the author may have a theme or themes in mind, but the readers bring their own insights, and in this case different readers may legitimately find different meanings based on patterns and messages in the text combined with their own interpretations and insights. But we seek for a balance between what is in the text and what the reader brings to the text. The message, however the reader interprets it, is always shaped by the author's intention and purpose.

Besides patterns in the story (which often point to the theme), there are certain parts of a story that often refer to the theme: the title, the beginning, and the very end. An important character's first and final words are also likely to carry powerful indications of theme.

In a story such as the *Odyssey,* which is long and complex and has a double plot—the story of Telemachus' search to find his father and the homeward journey of Odysseus, you will likely find multiple themes. But also try looking for a joining of the 2 plots with a single, overarching theme.

1. State the theme or themes you find as you continue reading the story. Explain how you concluded that these statements are thematic. When you have completed the story, review your answer, modifying it in the light of new evidence.

# Test 3: Books 9–12

## Essay Topics

1. Unlike the rest of the *Odyssey,* which is narrated by the poet/performer, Books 9–12 are narrated in the first person by Odysseus. What did you think of Homer's use of this technique?

2. Characterize the way Odysseus behaves with Anticleia; with Ajax.

3. As in many stories of giants, Polyphemus' power over Odysseus and his men comes from his brute strength. What resources does Odysseus draw on to overcome him? Compare and contrast this story with another story you know in which a "regular" person or child overcomes a giant.

4. Name the thing that Odysseus receives (or takes) from each of the following and how it helps him on his journey: Aeolus, Polyphemus, Circe, Tiresias.

5. Unlike Polyphemus and the Laestrygonians, the Sirens and Circe recognize Odysseus. What do you make of this?

6. Compare and contrast the world of Ithaca that Odysseus left and the world that Odysseus has lived in since.

7. How is the adventure on Helios' island similar to the adventures with Polyphemus and the Laestrygonians?

8. Predict what will happen next in the story.

# Book 13

## Journal and Discussion Topics

1. How does the narration change here?
2. In what way is Odysseus like a farmer?
3. Odysseus mentions his wife briefly in Book 13. Look back to locate other mentions of Penelope that Odysseus makes. What do you gather from the evidence you find?
4. What do you think of Zeus' response to Poseidon? Explain.
5. Why does Odysseus make up a story about his background?
6. What deceptions occur in Book 13?
7. Draw or find pictures to represent Odysseus before and after Athena's transformation of him.

## Summary

With the first line of Book 13, the poet/performer resumes narration. Alcinous, deeply impressed by Odysseus' tale, reiterates the request to his people for more gifts, which his kings/princes are anxious to supply. All retire for the night. The next morning, Alcinous offers a sacrifice, and Odysseus waits impatiently for the day to end. When the sun sets, Odysseus gives his blessing to all, asks that god grant he find his wife and everything he loves safe, and ends with a special blessing for Arete. The gifts for Odysseus are loaded onto the ship, and a bed prepared for him on the deck. As Odysseus sleeps, the ship carries him home, and still sleeping, he is lifted over the side and laid, with all his gifts, on a beach in Ithaca.

The Phaeacians, their mission accomplished, begin their journey home, but Poseidon complains to Zeus, saying he knew that Odysseus would get home someday, but not with so many gifts. Zeus responds that Poseidon may take whatever action he likes. Poseidon wants to both turn the ship to stone and block off the Phaeacian's port with a mountain, but Zeus persuades him not to put up the mountain. When Alcinous sees what Poseidon has done, he recognizes the doom that was prophesied to him, and he declares that the Phaeacians will no longer give passage to castaways and will attempt to propitiate Poseidon with a sacrifice so that he will not put a mountain around their city.

Odysseus, meanwhile, awakes and does not recognize where he is. While Athena protects him from recognition by a gray mist, Odysseus complains to himself that the Phaeacians have broken their promise, failing to take him home. He checks the treasure, and finds that it is all present and accounted for, but he weeps, longing for his home. At this point, Athena appears to him in the guise of a shepherd, and Odysseus begs her to identify the land and its people for him. She describes the land and identifies it as Ithaca. He, in turn, makes up a false history, claiming to be from Crete and to have fled his country after committing a murder. Athena then upbraids him, though half in jest, for his trickery, reveals her identity to him, and tells him that he will require patience and silence to get through the trials to come. Odysseus responds by criticizing Athena for ignoring him since he left Troy, and questions her truthfulness, asking if he is truly in Ithaca. Athena assures him that his wife is still waiting for him and that she, too, has waited, but that she did not wish to challenge Poseidon's authority. She then dispels the mist, allowing him to recognize his land, and he kisses the earth and prays in thanksgiving to the nymphs. Together, Athena and Odysseus hide Odysseus' treasure.

Athena then summarizes the situation at Odysseus' home: for 3 years the suitors have been courting Penelope while she waited only for Odysseus. Odysseus sees that he, like Agamemnon, might have met death on his return, and begs Athena to help him plan and to fight alongside him against the suitors. Athena promises to be with him and tells him that she foresees his victory. She tells him she will transform him so that he will seem to be an old man and no one will be able to recognize him. Then, she sends him to join his swineherd, while she goes to Sparta to call Telemachus home. She mentions that the suitors plot to murder Telemachus, and predicts that they will die instead. Then she touches Odysseus with her wand, and he turns into an old man. She gives him old, dirty, torn clothing and a staff, and they part.

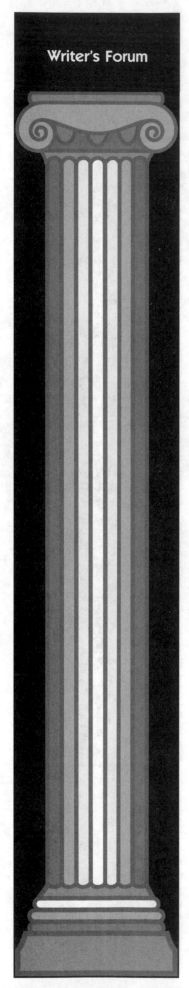

# Writer's Forum

### Description

In a piece of descriptive writing, you let the readers know about the attributes of something so they can picture it in their mind's eye. You choose the features you will mention based on what stands out among the physical properties and internal attributes of what you are describing, and these features will change depending on your topic. For example, if you were describing the setting of Alcinous' and Arete's palace, you might choose features such as "layout," and "decor." If, however, you were describing the character of Scylla, you would use different features: physical appearance, personality traits, actions, and habits. Here are some questions you can use to help you formulate your description:

- What is it that you wish to describe?
- What are its attributes?
- How is it apprehended by the senses—how does it look, smell, taste, feel, sound?
- How does it relate to other things in its environment or context?
- How can it be described by answering questions beginning

    Who?        When?
    What?       Why?
    Where?      How?

The way you organize the information you will use can vary depending on what you are describing. You can organize your description from

- top to bottom
- front to back
- side to side
- inside and outside

- around the perimeter
- from the beginning to the end of its cycle or process
- most important trait to least important (or vice versa)

Source words that can help you express concepts of similarity and difference include the following:

SIMILARITY

- also
- and
- as well as
- similarly

- besides
- furthermore
- likewise
- alike

- in addition
- too
- at the same time
- resemble

DIFFERENCE

- differ
- whereas
- however

- while
- but
- on the contrary

- conversely
- though
- on the other hand

1. Write a description of the spot where Odysseus awakes on the beach on the island of Ithaca. Then write a description of Odysseus' appearance after Athena transforms him. When you are done, write a brief reflection on the differences in content and organization between your 2 descriptions.

# Book 14

## Journal and Discussion Topics

**Note:** In this guide, Odysseus is called either "the beggar" or "Odysseus" while he is unrecognized, whichever seems most clear for the point being made.

1. Why do you think Odysseus tells Eumaeus the truth about some of what will happen as a result of Athena's plan, but then lies about his name and history?
2. Compare and contrast the made-up history Odysseus tells Alcinous with the one he tells Eumaeus.
3. Why is Eumaeus concerned about Telemachus?
4. What parts of Odysseus' description of himself (in his false Cretan history and in his description of meeting himself) do you think are accurate and which do you think don't hit the mark? Explain your judgment.
5. Why doesn't Eumaeus believe the beggar statements about Odysseus' homecoming?
6. Why won't Eumaeus accept the beggar's compact/bet?
7. How would you characterize Eumaeus?
8. Compare and contrast the two herdsmen, Polyphemus and Eumaeus.
9. What's the point of the beggar's story about Troy?
10. How do the ways the beggar addresses Eumaeus and Eumaeus addresses the beggar change through Book 14? What do you think this means?

## Summary

After Odysseus and Athena part, he goes to the hills where the swineherd (or forester) lives, far away from Odysseus' home. The forester is the one of Odysseus' field workers who cares the most about the estate. He had built himself a hut with a fence to protect it, and 12 sties within the yard to hold the sows, while the boars were allowed to roam, guarded by 4 dogs. When Odysseus approaches, Eumaeus is making himself a pair of shoes. The watchdogs catch sight of the beggar and run at him, and although he immediately sits down and drops his staff, they would have attacked him, had not Eumaeus dispersed them, yelling and throwing stones until they scatter. Then Eumaeus—introducing himself as a man who serves an absent master whom he loves, and connecting the beggar's condition as a wandering stranger with that of his master—invites the beggar in to eat first and talk after.

As they eat, Eumaeus summarizes the situation at his master's house, telling how the suitors are using up the estate, and Odysseus' thoughts turn to revenge. Odysseus, playing the role of the wanderer, asks the name of Eumaeus' master, saying he may have met this man during his roamings. Eumaeus responds by first making it clear that neither Penelope nor Telemachus will believe any news, and expresses his distrust of travelers who make up stories about having seen lost people in the hopes of getting a present for their news. That clear, he mentions the name of Odysseus, and the beggar replies that he knows this man is near at hand, but that he (the beggar) does not want and will not take anything for his news until the lord reenters his own home. Moreover, the beggar tells Eumaeus, his master will be avenged. Eumaeus does not believe

him and changes the subject, speaking briefly of his concern for Telemachus' ability to elude the suitors who lie in wait to kill him on his homeward journey, and then asking the beggar for his history.

Odysseus makes up a story that he is the illegitimate son of a wealthy man of Crete, whose jealous brothers gave him a very small part of their inheritance when their father died. His talents, however, gained him a wife from a rich family. After marrying, he spent his life at sea and at war, going to Troy and returning safely home. But one month after his return, he sailed for Egypt, where he and his crew were taken prisoner by the Egyptians, and he was spared only because he fell at the king's knees and begged him for asylum. He lived in Egypt 7 years, again growing rich, until a scheming Phoenician tricked him into accompanying him on a voyage. But when they were sailing to Libya, where the Phoenician planned to sell him, Zeus hit the ship with lightning, and the beggar was cast up on Thesprotia, where he was found by the king's son and taken in. It was there that he heard news of Odysseus, who had brought treasure to the king, and who was seeking to know if Zeus wanted him to return to Ithaca openly or secretly after so many years. Odysseus was preparing to journey home then, and the Thesprotians offered the man from Crete passage, too, but then stole his goods, gave him the rags he is now wearing, and tied him up while they landed at Ithaca. The Cretan managed to escape and get ashore.

Eumaeus hears him with pity, but clearly does not believe one word about Odysseus. He relates how he was once fooled by someone who claimed to have news of Odysseus. The beggar, in response, offers to make an agreement with Eumaeus: if Odysseus returns, Eumaeus will give the beggar new clothes and ship him home; if Odysseus does not return in the way the beggar has said, Eumaeus can order that the beggar be killed. Eumaeus points out that he could hardly face Zeus if he killed a guest, and changes the subject, pointing out that it is time for supper. Nevertheless, despite his expressed distrust of the beggar's news of Odysseus, Eumaeus has the best pig killed for their meal and offers the sacrifice, praying for Odysseus' return. He gives the beggar the choicest cuts, for which the beggar thanks him, calling him by name.

The beggar then tells a story to try to get someone to lend him a warm cloak for the night. He says that he was third in command after Odysseus and Menelaus at Troy, and one night he had left his cloak at camp, thinking the night would be warm, and so lay shivering while the other men slept. Getting Odysseus' attention, he told his situation, and Odysseus pretended that he'd had a prophetic dream that had to be relayed to Agamemnon. One of the young soldiers threw off his cloak and ran off to carry the news, and the beggar, comfortably wrapped in the castoff cloak, went to sleep. Eumaeus gets the point of the story, and promises that they'll see that he's warm at night. During the day, however, he must make do, because they don't have extras. Eumaeus promises that when Telemachus returns, he will give the beggar a new outfit and give him safe passage to whatever destination the beggar chooses. He sees the beggar comfortably settled, and goes himself to spend the night outside, protecting the herd, which shows Odysseus how loyal and dutiful Eumaeus is.

# Book 15

## Journal and Discussion Topics

1. What do you make of Athena's statement about women? Does she mean that Penelope is like that? Explain your thinking.
2. Do you personally agree with Menelaus' statement:
   "Measure is best in everything." (Fitzgerald, page 270)
   "In all things balance is better." (Lattimore, page 227)
   "The best rule is moderation in all things." (Rouse, page 170)
   "Balance is best in all things." (Fagles, page 321)
   Explain why you agree or disagree.
3. How is Nestor's idea of hospitality different from Menelaus' idea?
4. What role do you predict Theoclymenus will play in the story?
5. How does Odysseus test Eumaeus?
6. Why does Telemachus suggest that Theoclymenus go to Eurymachus and then send him to Peiraios?
7. How is the structure of this book different than that of any of the preceding books?
8. How do you imagine the meeting between Odysseus and Telemachus?

## Summary

The story now turns back to Athena's departure from Ithaca after Book 13. She travels to Sparta and tells Telemachus that he must return home immediately, saying that Penelope's father and kinsmen are urging her to marry Eurymachus, and suggesting that like all women with the prospect of a second husband, Penelope has no more care for the husband of her youth and her child by him. Thus, Telemachus should act alone, only finding one servant he can trust. Besides that, he must beware the suitors who are plotting to kill him. He can avoid death by following the route Athena tells him and spending his first night on Ithaca with the swineherd rather than going home, but he should send word to Penelope of his safe arrival. Telemachus is so eager to leave, that he immediately wakes Pisistratus, who tells him that they can't drive in the dark and should wait for Menelaus' gifts. When Telemachus hears Menelaus in the hall, he goes to him and bids him send them home, explaining that there is no one at home to guard his property. Menelaus understands, and has breakfast and parting gifts prepared. Menelaus gives him a goblet, prince Megapenthes gives a wine bowl, and Helen gives a gown that she embroidered for Telemachus' future bride.

On parting, Menelaus sends his good wishes to Nestor, and Telemachus wishes that he could bear those wishes as well to his father. At this, an eagle flies by carrying a goose in its talons, and Pisistratus bids Menelaus read the sign. It is Helen, however, who interprets the omen, saying that Odysseus, who may be home even on this day, will overcome the suitors. Pisistratus and Telemachus drive all day, sleeping at Pherai. The next day, Telemachus asks Pisistratus a favor: to leave him at the ship so that he can leave immediately, rather than taking him home to Nestor's house, where—out of kindness—Nestor

will detain him till the morrow. Knowing that Telemachus has read Nestor correctly, Pisistratus agrees and tells Telemachus to be off quickly.

As the crew prepares the ship and Telemachus makes his parting sacrifices, a stranger approaches him, the prophet Theoclymenos, who asks Telemachus who he is. Having heard the answer, Theoclymenos tells that he has killed a cousin, and begs passage on Telemachus' ship in order to avoid death. Telemachus welcomes him, and they board the ship. Athena sends a wind, and they are off.

Meanwhile, the beggar proposes to Eumaeus that he (the beggar) should take off for town and offer his services at Odysseus' house, performing some menial service. Eumaeus strongly urges him not to do so, telling him that the suitors are violent men, that they employ young, well-groomed servants, and adding that the beggar is no burden to them and should stay where he is until Telemachus comes. The beggar thanks him warmly and then changes the subject to ask about Odysseus' mother and father. Eumaeus responds that Odysseus' mother died of longing for her absent son and his father wishes for death, being heartbroken for the loss, both of his son and his wife. Eumaeus feels her loss deeply, too, because she raised him with her youngest child and treated him like a son in many ways, and now he is estranged from Penelope because of the suitors. This leads the beggar to ask Eumaeus his history, and dismissing anyone who doesn't care to hear the story, Eumaeus tells of being the son of Ktesios who ruled 2 towns on the island of Syrie. His nurse, a woman of Phoenicia, was seduced by some Phoenician sailors, and she offered to kidnap Eumaeus and give him to the Phoenicians to sell in return for their giving her passage to her home, from which she was kidnapped by pirates when she was a child. The woman dropped dead on the ship, and when they landed in Ithaca, Laertes purchased Eumaeus, and as the beggar observes, Eumaeus has led a good life since.

The story shifts back to Telemachus, just debarking from his ship and giving orders for the crew to moor her in town, while he travels overland. Theoclymenos asks what will become of him, and Telemachus responds that he cannot invite him home at the present and suggests that he go to Eurymachus (commentators say that this is sarcastic), who is likely to be Odysseus' inheritor as things look. Immediately a hawk flies by with a dove in its talons, and Theoclymenos interprets this as a sign that Telemachus' family will rule Ithaca forever. Telemachus then arranges for Theoclymenos to stay with someone he trusts, a member of his crew named Peiraios. The crew shoves off, and Telemachus sets off for Eumaeus' hut.

# Book 16

## Journal and Discussion Topics

1. What does Eumaeus' greeting to Telemachus tell you about Eumaeus' character?
2. Why is Telemachus upset when Eumaeus requests that he give the beggar his protection?
3. Why do you think Odysseus questions Telemachus about brothers when he knows Telemachus doesn't have any?
4. How many men must Odysseus and Telemachus take on?
5. Summarize Odysseus' plan.
6. How do the suitors react to the failure of their plan to kill Telemachus?
7. What new information makes the behavior of Antinous and Eurymachus seem even more blameworthy?

## Summary

After the beggar and Eumaeus have breakfast, the beggar hears the dogs greeting someone they know, and while he is telling Eumaeus, Telemachus comes into view. Eumaeus greets him lovingly, kissing him and embracing him as if he were his own son who had been gone 10 years and escaped death. Telemachus asks whether his mother has married, and Eumaeus assures him that she is still at home, grieving for Odysseus. As Telemachus enters the hut, the beggar moves to yield his seat, but Telemachus stops him and has Eumaeus build another seat for him. Eumaeus then serves them, and Telemachus asks Eumaeus about the beggar's background. Eumaeus says briefly that the man is a Cretan just escaped from the Thesprotians and that he wishes Telemachus' protection. Telemachus finds the idea ironic—he has neither the age, the training, nor the honor to give protection. He will, however, undertake to give the beggar clothes, a broadsword, sandals, and passage on a ship to anywhere he wants to go. Telemachus regrets that he cannot invite the beggar home with him because of the suitors. The beggar responds by saying that Telemachus' situation causes him pain and asking if Telemachus has no brothers or kin to support him in opposing the behavior of the suitors. Telemachus explains that he has no brothers; that and his young age are what make him unable to defend his household. He then orders Eumaeus to go to Penelope and secretly tell her that Telemachus has returned home safely. Eumaeus asks if he should go to Laertes as well, but Telemachus tells him to come straight back, sending Penelope's housekeeper (Eurynome) with the message to Laertes.

As soon as Eumaeus leaves, Athena appears in the yard, visible only to Odysseus. She tells him that the time has come to reveal himself to his son and that she will join them in the battle against the suitors. Using her wand again, she transforms Odysseus, making him young and clean shaven. Telemachus thinks that a god has come to him. Odysseus reveals his identity and weeping, embraces Telemachus, but Telemachus insists that a god must have transformed him. Odysseus chides him, but explains that Athena transformed him.

Now Telemachus hugs his father and cries, and Odysseus weeps with him. Curious, Telemachus asks how Odysseus returned to Ithaca, and Odysseus

tells him how the Phaeacians gave him passage. He then asks Telemachus to enumerate the suitors so they may know how many men they have to kill, for Athena has a plan. Telemachus tells of 108 suitors, 8 retainers, and Medon the crier and the harper (the last 2 will turn out to be loyal to Odysseus), for a total of 118. Odysseus promises his son that Athena and Zeus will fight with them and then gives him instructions. At daybreak the following morning, Telemachus is to go down to town and mingle with the suitors. Eumaeus will bring Odysseus along in his beggar's guise. Odysseus warns Telemachus not to react if the suitors are cruel to him. When Athena signals to Odysseus, Odysseus will in turn signal Telemachus that it is time to remove all weapons from the hall, and he tells Telemachus to answer any queries by saying that he wants to move them out of the smoke and prevent the suitors from hurting each other when they're drunk. Telemachus must keep out only 2 swords, 2 spears, and 2 shields for Telemachus and Odysseus to use. Then Odysseus swears Telemachus to secrecy about his arrival because he knows that they need to find out which of the women and which of the men are loyal, and which are corrupt.

As Odysseus and Telemachus are talking at the hut, Eumaeus and a crewman from Telemachus' ship both arrive at the same time to inform Penelope that Telemachus is safely home. Eumaeus delivers his message in secret, as he was requested, but the crewman blurts out the news, letting the suitors who remained in the house know that their plan has failed. The suitors go down to the beach to meet the ship sailed by the would-be murderers. Antinous can't explain how Telemachus got past them, but leaves it to the group assembled to plan Telemachus' death; he reasons that Telemachus must now know of the plot and thinks that if Telemachus informs the assembly, all the suitors may be exiled. Amphinomus is the only one who speaks against killing Telemachus; he suggests they consult Zeus, and this convinces the others to wait for a sign and follow the gods' design.

Meanwhile, Penelope, having had the plot to murder Telemachus confirmed to her by Medon, goes down to the suitors. She chastises Antinous, reminding him that Odysseus took in Antinous' father when he was a supplicant and no one else would help him. Eurymachus responds with glib lies, telling her that just as Odysseus used to take him on his knee, so he feels tenderly toward Telemachus and would never think to harm Telemachus, as no man there would. Penelope leaves them and goes to her room to weep for Odysseus. Athena grants her sleep and then returns to Odysseus and Telemachus, restoring the guise of the beggar before Eumaeus reaches his home. When Eumaeus appears, Telemachus asks him for news of the suitors, but Eumaeus had hurried back and seen nothing except a ship with many oarsmen and spears, which he took to be the suitors returning from their ambush.

## Essay Topics

1. Compare and contrast Penelope's wait for Odysseus to come home and Odysseus' wait to be able to return home.

2. Read the quotations below. Then think about and answer the following question: How does the theme of weaving connect Penelope, Athena, and Odysseus?

   Fitzgerald: "Weave me a way to pay them back." (page 242)

   Lattimore: "Come then, weave the design, the way I shall take my vengeance." (page 208)

   Rouse: "Come on, weave me a plan to punish them. . . ." (page 156)

   Fagles: "Come, weave us a scheme so I can pay them back." (page 299)

3. What do you think of the plot to kill the suitors as Odysseus has explained it? Be specific.

4. What has been the most moving moment in the story so far for you? Explain why.

5. Can you believe that Odysseus could come to Ithaca and make no attempt to see Penelope? Explain your reasoning.

6. What loose ends are there left to tie up in the story for the ending to be satisfactory in your opinion?

# Book 17

## Journal and Discussion Topics

1. What do you gather from Telemachus' and Odysseus' first interaction in Book 17?
2. How does Theoclymenos' presence add to the story?
3. What does Homer's comment on Medon's relationship with the suitors suggest to you?
4. What qualities of character does Odysseus' reaction to Melanthius show?
5. How did the episode with Argos affect you?
6. What do you think of Athena's advice to Odysseus about begging from the suitors?
7. When Odysseus is begging from Antinous, why do you think he makes up a false story to tell him?
8. What do you think Homer achieved by the interaction of Odysseus and Antinous in Book 17?
9. What does Penelope learn about the disguised Odysseus from his communication to her through Eumaeus?
10. What is your favorite part of Book 17?

## Summary

Telemachus announces that he is going to show himself to his mother so she won't be worried. He bids Eumaeus to take the beggar to town with him, whether the beggar wishes it or not. Odysseus agrees amicably. Telemachus leaves and is greeted at the house, first by Eurycleia and some other servants, and then by his mother, who asks him for news. But instead of answering her request, he sends her to bathe and pray for revenge, and he leaves to meet Theoclymenos. He avoids the suitors, but joins Mentor, Antiphus, and Halitherses and tells them his story. Peiraios arrives with Theoclymenos and tells Telemachus to send his maids over to collect the presents from Menelaus. Telemachus replies that he is in danger from the suitors, and should he die, he wants Peiraios to have the gifts; if, however, the suitors are vanquished, then will be the time for Peiraios to send the gifts to him.

Telemachus takes Theoclymenos home with him, and after they have eaten, Penelope asks what news he has heard of Odysseus on his journey. He tells her that Nestor knew nothing, but Menelaus both predicted Odysseus' triumphant return and had heard that Odysseus was prisoner on the island of Calypso. Theoclymenos interjects that he has more information—Odysseus is now present on Ithaca and will bring doom upon the suitors.

During this conversation, the suitors are taking part in athletic games, until Medon calls them to lunch. At the same time, Eumaeus and Odysseus are making their way toward town. Odysseus asks Eumaeus for a staff, which he supplies, and Eumaeus, all the while thinking he leads a beggar, leads his master home. On the way, they meet the goatherd, Melanthius, who jeers at Odysseus and kicks him. Odysseus does not respond, but Eumaeus prays aloud for Odysseus' return.

Melanthius, after a few more insults, leaves to join the suitors. Eumaeus and Odysseus agree that Eumaeus will enter the hall first, and Odysseus will follow. Eumaeus warns him to come soon, or he may get beaten, but Odysseus responds that he is used to such treatment. In response to Odysseus' voice, a dog, left to die on the dung pile by the gate, lifts his head. Odysseus sees him and recognizes his hunting dog, Argos. He weeps at the sight. As Eumaeus enters the house, Argos dies.

Telemachus notices Eumaeus' entrance and calls him over, giving him food for Odysseus, but also sending a message through him that Odysseus should approach the suitors to beg from them. The harper plays while Odysseus eats, and then Athena appears to Odysseus, telling him to try the suitors to learn their characters, although she says that all will die. Odysseus begins begging, and Melanthius informs the company that the beggar came to town in company with Eumaeus. Antinous attacks Eumaeus for bringing the beggar who will only help to eat up Odysseus' estate. Eumaeus begins an answer, but stops at a look from Telemachus, who sarcastically thanks Antinous for showing such concern over the estate and then bids Antinous give the beggar food. Antinous pulls out his footstool as a gift to the beggar, and the other suitors give food. But when Odysseus asks Antinous for food, explaining that he once was prosperous and telling a story of how he came to his present poor circumstances, Antinous interrupts him and sends him out to the passage. Odysseus responds that Antinous would not even be giving his own food if he donated something to Odysseus, since he is living off someone else's property, and Antinous responds by throwing the footstool at him, hitting his shoulder. Odysseus keeps walking, but criticizes Antinous for hitting a man because he is hungry. One of the suitors joins in rebuking Antinous, but Antinous does not care. Telemachus, Penelope, and Eurynome all feel for the beggar, and Penelope sends Eumaeus to bring the man to her, for she hopes for news of Odysseus. Eumaeus tells her that the beggar does, in fact, claim to have news of Odysseus. Penelope prays again that Odysseus will gain revenge. Just then, Telemachus sneezes, a good omen, at which Penelope tells Eumaeus that she will give the man new clothes if he has told the truth. Eumaeus delivers the message, but the beggar— citing the suitors' reputation and Antinous' behavior to him—insists on waiting till sundown (when the suitors are not present). At first Penelope blames the beggar for not coming, but when Eumaeus explains, she sees the wisdom of his plan and acquiesces.

Eumaeus must return to the swine, and he tells Telemachus, who warns him to be careful. Telemachus instructs him to eat before he goes and return at dawn with animals for a meal.

# STRATEGY 15            Irony

*Directions:
Read the explanation, then complete the exercises.*

**Irony** comes from a Greek word meaning "someone who hides under a false appearance." When irony is used, things appear different, even the opposite, of what they really are; unexpected events happen; what people say is not what they mean. Authors use irony to create interest, surprise, or an understanding with their readers that the characters do not share. There are three types of irony.

**Verbal irony** is irony in the use of language. Verbal irony means that what is said can be understood differently from, or the opposite of, what is meant. For example, when Polyphemus says "Nohbdy tricked me" or "Nobody/Noman is killing me," his understanding (what he means) is completely different than the understanding of the other Cyclops and the reader, creating irony. Irony also occurs when someone intentionally says something that can be taken 2 ways, knowing that the hearer will choose the wrong interpretation—this is also known as equivocation.

In **dramatic irony** there is knowledge that the author or narrator makes available to the reader, but the characters are unaware of it. When the poet/performer tells us in Book 1 that all Odysseus' shipmates will die and we hear shortly afterward that it is the will of Zeus that Odysseus return home, this creates dramatic irony for every incident up till Book 13, when Odysseus finally knows that he is in Ithaca. For all this time, we know and the narrator knows, but Odysseus doesn't know, that he will actually be allowed to return to his homeland. Another example: it is ironic when Eumaeus leads his master home, thinking he is bringing a beggar.

**Situational irony** can occur either from the point of view of a character or the reader. You get situational irony when something that is expected with a great deal of certainty doesn't happen (this can be from either point of view) or when something that is intended fails to materialize (this is only possible from a character's point of view, except in Choose-Your-Own Adventures or other books in which the reader participates by making a choice). When Alcinous and the Phaeacians have been so gracious to Odysseus, following Zeus' desire that people care for strangers, we may expect that Zeus will reward them. The more they do for Odysseus, the more we may expect that Zeus will show some appreciation. Instead they are punished—their magic ship and its crew are turned to stone before their eyes. This is an ironic twist that ends their tradition of generosity to wanderers and beggars. The suitors experience situational irony when their ambush fails and they find, to their amazement, that Telemachus has circumvented them and reached Ithaca alive.

1. Keep a record of other examples of irony in this story as you review books you've already read and as you continue to read.

# Book 18

## Journal and Discussion Topics

1. The nickname of Irus is a joke on Iris, the female deity of the rainbow who carried messages for the Gods. Explain the joke.
2. What is Odysseus trying to tell Amphinomus?
3. What do you think of Odysseus' farewell to Penelope before he left for Troy?
4. Why do you think Odysseus spoke to the maids as he did?
5. How do you feel about Amphinomus' fate given how he acts?
6. Draw a picture of Penelope among the suitors or the gifts the suitors brought her.

## Summary

Irus, the town beggar, enters the hall and challenges Odysseus' right to be there, offering to fight him. Odysseus offers to share the door slab, and warns Irus not to press him, or he may fight. Irus is angered and demands satisfaction. Antinous declares a prize of a pudding, the right to eat with the suitors from now on, and the right to be the only beggar in the hall. Odysseus asks them to swear that they will not assist Irus, and Telemachus assures him that the fight will be fair. Athena enhances Odysseus' looks as he prepares to fight, and by the time they are ready to begin, Irus is terrified. Odysseus hits him one blow, breaking his jaw bone, and drags him out by his ankle to keep guard by the gate. Returning to his doorstep, he finds the suitors greet him kindly. Antinous brings him the pudding, and Amphinomus gives him loaves and wine in a golden cup. Odysseus is moved to warn Amphinomus, telling him that the master of the house will return seeking vengeance, and urging him to leave. But Athena prevents his leaving, and we are told that he will die from a spear thrown by Telemachus.

Penelope is suddenly moved by Athena (although she doesn't realize that this is the cause) to go down to the suitors and show herself. Before she goes, Athena casts a sleep upon her and enhances her beauty. When she awakes, she goes to the hall with her 2 maids, and all the suitors are filled with desire for her. She goes to Telemachus and chastises him for permitting the beggar to be treated badly in their hall. Telemachus answers her respectfully, acknowledging the justice of what she says, and telling her that the beggar has bested Irus. Eurymachus interrupts to praise Penelope's beauty, but she replies that her looks were lost when her husband left for Troy. She then tells them Odysseus' parting message to her: that she should take care of the house and his parents; but when Telemachus grows so that his beard is dark, if Odysseus has not returned, she should remarry. She indicates that she will remarry, though she has no wish to, but she complains that the suitors do not show her due respect, using up her property rather than giving her gifts. Odysseus is pleased with her ploy, and the suitors all send for gifts for her. Penelope retires to her quarters and her maids bring the treasures behind her.

Meanwhile, night falls, and the maids take turns tending the fire. Odysseus goes to them and offers to relieve them of this duty, and Melantho, Melanthius' sister and Eurymachus' lover, insults Odysseus. He responds that if Telemachus

heard her, he would cut off her arms and legs. The women run away, frightened by him, and he takes up the job of tending the hearth. The suitors, however, continue to mock him, Eurymachus in particular, offering to hire him to clear wasteland of stones. Odysseus replies that if the 2 of them were to scythe, plow, or fight with spears, Eurymachus would change his attitude. Eurymachus, angered, takes his footstool and throws it, but Odysseus ducks and the stool hits one of the wine stewards on the hand. Telemachus suggests that they are drunk and should go home—whenever it suits them, of course. The suitors begin to grow angry, but Amphinomus seconds Telemachus, suggesting that they go away and leave the beggar to Telemachus' care, and they do.

# Book 19

## Journal and Discussion Topics

1. Compare and contrast Odysseus' instructions to Telemachus about the weapons in Book 16 with his instructions to Telemachus in Book 19 and with what Telemachus actually says and does about the weapons.
2. Odysseus doesn't answer Penelope's first questions right off. Why do you think he proceeds the way he does?
3. What explanation could there be for Penelope confiding in a strange beggar?
4. After Odysseus finishes telling Penelope his made-up story, Homer says
   A. "Now all these lies he made appear so truthful/she wept as she sat listening." (Fitzgerald, page 360)
   B. "Falsehoods all, but he gave his falsehoods all the ring of truth. As she listened on, her tears flowed." (Fagles, page 397)
   C. "He made his long invention seem just like the truth as he told it; and her tears flowed while she listened." (Rouse, page 217)
   D. "He knew how to say many false things that were like true sayings. As she listened her tears ran. . . ." (Lattimore, page 287)
   Why do you think Homer makes this point?
5. When does Odysseus begin speaking the truth?
6. What hints do the women have that this beggar is Odysseus before Eurycleia recognizes him?
7. Why do you think Homer spends so much time on the story of the origin of Odysseus' scar?
8. Why does Odysseus speak so harshly to Eurycleia?
9. Why doesn't Odysseus need Eurycleia's insight into the maids' characters?
10. Is Penelope planning to marry a suitor or not? Explain your thinking.

## Summary

The suitors gone, Odysseus speaks openly to Telemachus, reminding him to move the arms. When Telemachus tells Eurycleia to lock the women in their quarters so that he can put the arms away, she is pleased to see his interest in his father's arms. But she asks who will bear a light for him. Telemachus says that the beggar will, and his tone prevents Eurycleia from voicing any objection. As they work, Telemachus sees a change in the light, and recognizes the presence of a god; it is Athena. Odysseus sends Telemachus to bed, and prepares to test Penelope and her maids, who soon come down to the hall. Melantho again harasses Odysseus, accusing him of lusting after the maids. He responds that he is in his present condition because he is down on his luck, and warns her to beware lest Penelope grow angry, Odysseus return, or Telemachus, who is now too old to be fooled by their tricks, take power. Penelope, overhearing, chastises Melantho, and tells her that her life will be forfeit. Penelope then turns her attention to the beggar, instructing Eurynome prepare a bench for him and asking him his name and origins.

Odysseus replies by praising Penelope herself and her fame and requesting that she not insist that he tell of his family and home because it is too

painful. Penelope responds that she lost her looks when Odysseus left for Troy and that the focus of her life is longing for his return. She confesses the ruse of the loom—her claim that she had to weave a shroud for Laertes before she wed, while all the time she unraveled her work at night until she was caught and forced to finish. And now she is having a difficult time avoiding marriage, and her parents and son, she says, wish her to remarry. Having confided in the beggar, she requests his confidence in return, and asks again about his family background. After repeating how painful it is to him to tell it, the beggar begins another story of his Cretan heritage, and tells how he hosted Odysseus when Odysseus was on his way to Troy and was blown to Crete by a gale. These lies make Penelope weep, but although he feels deeply, the beggar gives no sign. Penelope asks for proof, and the beggar describes the clothes Odysseus (supposedly) wore, and a brooch, and his herald. Penelope weeps again and says she will never see Odysseus again. The beggar says it is natural to weep for her husband, but that he has something true to say to her: Odysseus is on his way home. In a mix of truth and fiction, he then tells her that Odysseus will come within the next 24 hours. Penelope, still denying that she will ever see Odysseus again, calls her maids to wash the beggar and make a bed for him. The beggar, however, declines the comfort of a bed with covers and says he doesn't want a footbath from the maids—only if there is some old and trusted servant, he will let her wash his feet. Penelope calls Eurycleia and asks her to bathe the beggar's feet (the different versions render this line differently, but all except Lattimore create the expectation that Odysseus has been identified by Penelope, only to negate it). Eurycleia addresses a passage to the absent (she thinks) Odysseus, and then tells the beggar how like Odysseus he seems. The beggar responds that she is not the first to notice a similarity between the 2 men, but he suddenly remembers his scar, and as soon as he does, Eurycleia touches it and knows him.

In a digression, we learn the history of the scar. Just after Odysseus was born, Anticleia's father came to visit Ithaca to name his grandson, promising him gifts when he grew older. When Odysseus went to collect the gifts, the men took him hunting, and Odysseus killed a wild boar, but was gored in the leg. Eurycleia announces her discovery to Odysseus, and looks toward Penelope to tell her, but she is not paying attention, and Odysseus grabs Eurycleia and tells her under his breath to keep her discovery secret or he'll kill her. She insists that he can trust her, and offers to tell him which maids are trustworthy and which are not, but he says he already knows. When the washing is done, Penelope tells the beggar her dream of an eagle killing her geese, and the eagle telling her that he is Odysseus and the geese are the suitors. The beggar tells her that the dream has already been interpreted by Odysseus. Then Penelope announces that on the following day she will have a contest in which 12 axe heads are set up and whoever can string Odysseus' bow and shoot an arrow through the 12 axes, she will marry. The beggar promises that Odysseus will be present for the trial. And Penelope replies that she could stay awake forever, if only the beggar would keep her company, and commending the beggar to rest wherever he chooses, she goes to bed and weeps for her husband until Athena puts her to sleep.

# Writer's Forum

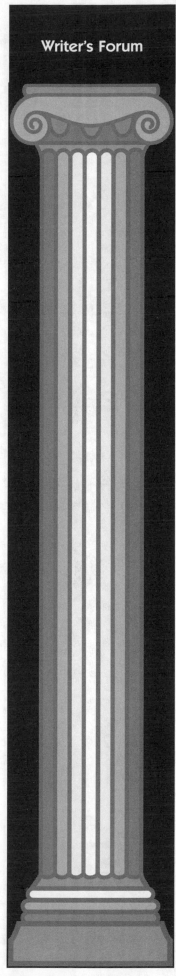

An anecdote is a short, self-contained, interesting or humorous story. Like any other narrative, an anecdote has a plot with a beginning, middle, and end. It also generally has characters, sometimes even a main character. But unlike most narratives, it often does not have a well-developed setting, and very little, if any, character development. Also, unlike other types of narratives, it is likely to have a moral or a punchline, or some other fairly explicit way of stating what the point is. And, there usually isn't much room for interpretation of that point.

Anecdotes are used frequently in conversation. In writing, they are often used at the beginning of an essay or similar work to help attract and focus the reader's attention, or within the body of the work to illustrate a point. Homer sometimes uses them to give additional information on something happening in the story.

In Book 19, Homer uses an anecdote to tell the story of Odysseus' scar. Look back at this anecdote and notice how it is similar to and different from longer narratives.

1. Write an anecdote explaining one of the following:

   A. The name *Calypso* means "the concealer." Make up an explanation of how the goddess got her name.
   B. Tell how the wolves and/or mountain lions escaped from Circe.
   C. Recount what happened when the other Cyclops met Polyphemus for the first time after Odysseus escaped.
   D. Make up an anecdote about how Odysseus got the idea of the Trojan Horse as a way of getting soldiers into the walled city of Troy.

# Book 20

## Journal and Discussion Topics

1. What do the similes used to describe Odysseus as he lies sleepless convey to you?
2. How is trust important in Book 20?
3. Why do you think Telemachus criticizes Penelope to Eurycleia?
4. How is the suitors' preparation of their meal different from the meal preparation in Nestor's and Menelaus' houses?
5. Characterize the change in Telemachus that takes place in this book.
6. Why do you think Athena wanted Odysseus insulted by the suitors?
7. Why is the suitors' criticism of Telemachus ironic?
8. How does Homer's use of omens strike you?

## Summary

Odysseus makes his bed in the entranceway, and lying awake, hears a group of the maids slip out to go to the suitors. He debates whether to kill them on the spot, and decides to wait. But still he lies sleepless, trying to figure out how he can fight such a crowd. Athena comes to him and asks what is troubling him. He tells her, and she sarcastically praises his faith, telling him to trust her and go to sleep. He does, but Penelope is awake, weeping and praying to Artemis and saying she saw an image of Odysseus that seemed real. Odysseus wakes and goes outdoors where he prays to Zeus for a sign, and Zeus gives him a peal of thunder, and lets him hear the prayer of one of the maids who grinds the grain and barley, and who, upon hearing the thunder, asks Zeus that this might be the last day the suitors feast in the hall.

Next, Telemachus wakes and calls to Eurycleia to see how the guest is treated, accusing Penelope of neglecting him. Eurycleia chides him for speaking so of his mother and tells him that the beggar received whatever he wished. Telemachus then goes to the square with his lance, and Eurycleia sends the maids to work. Eumaeus arrives, and asks if Odysseus is still being poorly treated by the suitors, and Odysseus admits that it is so. Melanthius then comes with his herds, and rebukes the beggar for not leaving. The cattleman, Philoetius, joins them in the square as well, asks Eumaeus who the beggar is, and greets him shaking his hand, saying that he recognizes a noble bearing in him, and that when he looks upon him he remembers Odysseus. The beggar responds that if Philoetius wishes, he can see Odysseus' return, which is imminent. The cattleman shows his willingness to join in a fight, and Eumaeus seconds it. Meanwhile, the suitors, out in the field, are again plotting to murder Telemachus, when they see an omen—an eagle clutching a rockdove in its talons. Upon seeing this, Amphinomus says the plan is unlucky, and urges them to think of food, so they all head for the hall.

While Eumaeus and Philoetius help serve, Telemachus gives the beggar a seat by the door sill, and publicly warns the suitors to let the beggar be or they will have to deal with him (Telemachus). Antinous urges the other suitors to accept Telemachus' dictum for the moment, since they have had a bad omen from Zeus. Public heralds begin parading through Ithaca, leading animals for the sacrifice to Apollo. Athena desires that Odysseus be offended again, and the suitor Ktesippos throws a cow's foot at him, which Odysseus ducks. Telemachus says bluntly that if it had struck the beggar, he would have killed Ktesippos, and warns the others to behave in his house, making it clear to them that he knows of their murderous plotting. One of the suitors, Agelaus, urges the others to let the beggar be, but also urges Telemachus to accept the "fact" of his father's death and urge his mother to accept marriage with the man who has given the most gifts, allowing Telemachus to enjoy his patrimony. Telemachus responds that he has not stood in the way of her marriage, but has offered additional dowry to her; but he will not send her away against her will. Athena makes the suitors laugh at this, and Theoclymenos sees a vision of them dying and making their way into the underworld. When he tells them, they continue to laugh, so he leaves to return to Peiraios. The suitors continue to denigrate the beggar, and Telemachus watches Odysseus, waiting for a signal. Penelope sets her chair to look on Telemachus and the beggar and watches, and the poet/performer tells us that the suitors' supper will be what Athena and Odysseus prepare for them.

**Essay Topics**

1. Enumerate the attacks that Odysseus has endured in his homeland. What function do they serve? How do they compare to the attacks during the wanderings?

2. How has Odysseus become "Nobody"?

3. It could be argued that Odysseus is responsible for the recognitions that occur with Eurycleia and among the Phaeacians. Give evidence to support this claim.

4. What would you do if you were in Penelope's situation?

5. What do you think will happen in the contest of the bow?

6. How do you think Odysseus will make himself known to Penelope?

7. Discuss the complexities of re-establishing a relationship with someone you haven't seen or heard from in 20 years.

# Book 21

## Journal and Discussion Topics

1. How does Homer keep the reader's focus on the bow as a weapon while preparations are being made for the contest?
2. What do you think Penelope THINKS will be the result of the contest? What do you think she HOPES will happen?
3. Why do you think Telemachus laughs? Why does he say what he does afterwards?
4. Why doesn't Telemachus string the bow? Explain your answer.
5. Do you think Antinous' idea of heating and greasing the bow is cheating? Explain your answer.
6. What is the purpose of the 4 instructions Odysseus gives Eumaeus and Philoetius? How are they carried out?
7. Do you think Antinous tried the bow? What in the text led to your conclusion?
8. What is Antinous' plan, when it is clear that the suitors cannot string the bow?
9. Why do you think Telemachus speaks as he does when Penelope is making arrangements for "the beggar" to try the bow?
10. What was the effect on you of Homer's comparing Odysseus to a harper?
11. Predict what will happen in Book 22.

## Summary

Athena awakens Penelope, who goes to fetch the bow from a storeroom. The bow was a gift from Iphitos who was killed by Heracles, and Odysseus kept it in his home as a keepsake rather than take it to Troy. Penelope weeps as she lifts down the bow and takes it to the suitors. Her maids follow with the axeheads and other equipment for the contest. Both Eumaeus and Philoetius weep as Eumaeus lays the bow at the suitors' feet, and Antinous jeers at them. All of a sudden Telemachus laughs, but he quickly berates himself for showing such an inappropriate emotion. He then says he would like to try the bow himself, but instead busies himself preparing the row of axeheads. Then he tries the bow. On the fourth attempt, he is about to string it when a look from Odysseus warns him off, and he pretends to curse himself and offers the bow to the suitors to try.

Leodes, the only one of the suitors who was disgusted by the manners of the others, tries first and fails. Antinous then has Melanthius light a fire and declares that future contenders shall heat and grease the bow to make it more pliable. While all the other suitors try, Antinous and Eurymachus wait.

Meanwhile, Odysseus follows Eumaeus and Philoetius into the hall and asks them if they would stand by Odysseus if he returned, to which they both respond by praying for his return. Odysseus reveals himself, promising them wives and cattle if with Zeus' help they can kill the suitors. He shows them the scar on his thigh to prove his identity, and both men recognize him. They all embrace and weep, till Odysseus cuts them off, and gives them their orders: They are to return to the contest separately. When it is time for Odysseus to have the bow, Eumaeus is to defy the suitors and bring it to him. Then Eumaeus

must tell the women to lock their door, and no matter what they hear, not to come out, but to continue weaving. At the same time, Philoetius is to lock the outer gate and lash the crossbar in place.

As they return to the courtyard, Eurymachus is trying unsuccessfully to string the bow. He says he is humiliated because the suitors cannot measure up to the standard set by Odysseus. Antinous replies that it is a holy day, and they should leave the bow and axes till the next day and try tomorrow after making sacrifices to Apollo, the patron god of archers. A meal is served, and during it the beggar speaks, praising Antinous' suggestion to leave the trial, and asking for a chance to take the challenge of the bow. Antinous suggests that the beggar is drunk and tells him to leave the bow for his betters. But Penelope intervenes and chastises Antinous for discourtesy to Telemachus' guest, saying that even if the stranger drew the bow he cannot imagine that he could take Penelope as his bride. Eurymachus replies that they don't imagine that, but that people would make fun of the suitors if the beggar could string the bow when they couldn't. Penelope says Eurymachus has no reputation to lose, and she will reward the stranger with clothes, a lance, a broadsword, and an escort if he strings the bow.

Telemachus intervenes and claims to be the sole authority on who may handle the bow, even if he chooses to give it to the beggar as a gift. He sends Penelope to her room, and she goes, weeping for Odysseus until Athena grants her sleep. At the same time, Eumaeus, following Odysseus' earlier instruction, has retrieved the bow and is making for Odysseus when the crowd in the hall starts shouting at him. In his confusion, he puts down the bow, while Telemachus yells to him to take the bow to his guest and threatens to stone him if he obeys the suitors. The suitors break into laughter at Telemachus' speech, and Eumaeus quickly takes the bow and quiver to Odysseus at the door, and then gives Eurycleia instructions to lock the door to the women's quarters and warn them not to come out, no matter what they hear. She follows the directions while Philoetius locks and lashes the courtyard gate and Odysseus checks the bow. Then, in a passage in which Odysseus is compared to a harper, Homer tells how Odysseus easily and smoothly strings his bow, and Zeus immediately lets out a peal of thunder. Odysseus laughs to himself, picks up an arrow, and shoots it cleanly through the axeheads, telling Telemachus that his guest has not disgraced him. He nods to his son, who belts on his sword, takes his spear, and stands ready by his father.

# STRATEGY 16

## Foreshadowing and Flashback

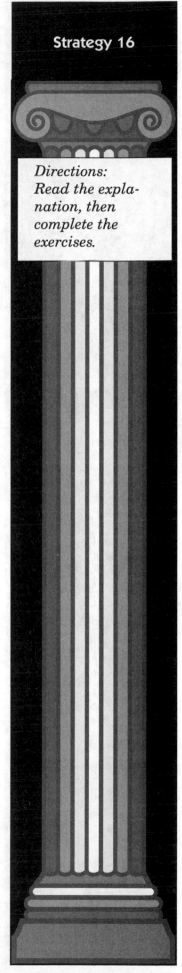

*Directions: Read the explanation, then complete the exercises.*

Writers do not always tell plot events in chronological order. One technique they may use is to hint at events before their place in the sequence. This is called **foreshadowing,** and it lets readers know beforehand something about what is going to happen later. This technique helps create suspense and keeps the reader involved in the unfolding plot. Foreshadowing usually creates dramatic irony because it gives the reader knowledge that the characters do not have.

Foreshadowing may come from a character, from the setting, or from the narrator. For example, when Odysseus first describes the sleeping Cyclops using words like *savage, brute, grim, lawless, monstrous* (depending on the translation), you may conclude that the upcoming adventure will put Odysseus and his men in danger. The description of the setting in Alcinous' and Arete's palace is another example of foreshadowing. The gracious and beautiful palace suggests that Odysseus will be received by gracious and hospitable people. When the narrator tells us that Odysseus could not save his men, on the first page of Book 1, this is a foreshadowing of the death of Odysseus' shipmates.

Writers may also go back to material that happened prior to the beginning of the story or earlier in the plot sequence. This is called **flashback.** Flashbacks give the reader necessary background material for understanding the story. Flashbacks may come from the narrator or the characters. When Odysseus narrates his adventures to the Phaeacians in Books 9 to 12, this is a very long flashback. When Homer tells the story of Odysseus' scar, it is a shorter flashback.

1. Find another example of a flashback. What essential information does it contain?

2. Find 3 different examples of foreshadowing from omens. What conclusions did you draw from them while you were reading?

3. Besides omens, in what ways does Homer foreshadow the death of the suitors?

# Book 22

## Journal and Discussion Topics

1. What do you think of Eurymachus' analysis of the blame for the situation at Odysseus' house and his proposal to Odysseus? What do you think of Odysseus' response? Explain your answers.
2. What is the value of the bow at the beginning of the fight? Why are arms necessary afterwards?
3. The poet and the crier are both spared. How is each like Odysseus?
4. What do you think of the descriptions of the deaths of the suitors?
5. In Book 19, Odysseus tells Eurycleia that she needn't tell him about the maids' characters because he can see them for himself. But in Book 22, he asks for her analysis. How do you explain this?
6.. How is the contest of the bow similar to the discus contest on Scheria for Odysseus?
7. What do you think Odysseus is feeling as the serving women greet him at the very end of this book?

## Summary

The beggar gets rid of his rags and takes his stand on the doorsill, but he is not recognized when, invoking Apollo, he kills the unsuspecting "ringleader" of the suitors, Antinous, piercing him with an arrow through the throat. The suitors, attributing the death to accident, still immediately threaten the beggar and seek for weapons to avenge "the best in Ithaca" . . . and discover that those weapons that had hung in the hall are gone. Then Odysseus declares himself, not by name, but by ownership of what the suitors have tried to take for their own. Eurymachus attempts a compromise, implicating the dead Antinous (truly or falsely) in a plot to gain the kingship of Ithaca, with or without Penelope, and by Telemachus' death, if necessary. Odysseus does not accept the offer to restore his lost property with additional gifts, and challenges the suitors to fight him or run—if they think they can escape. Eurymachus responds by telling the suitors to draw the swords they wear on their belts, use their tables as shields, and charge Odysseus as a group. As he leads them in an attack, Odysseus shoots an arrow into his chest. Amphinomus attacks Odysseus with a sword in an attempt to clear the doorway, but Telemachus hits him with a spear. Telemachus realizes that the 4 defenders need to arm. He hurries to Odysseus to make the suggestion, and Odysseus agrees, telling him to run because when his arrows are gone, he will be vulnerable. When Telemachus returns, he and the 2 servants arm and join Odysseus by the door. Odysseus uses the bow until he is out of arrows, and then arms himself.

Now Odysseus has Eumaeus stand in the passage outside the hall to guard it. At the same time, one of the suitors spots the window in the hall that lights the passage and suggests that one of them climb through and run to town for help. Melanthius suggests that it would be a better plan for him to climb through and get the arms out of the storage chamber, where he is sure they are hidden. He secures 12 shields, spears, and helmets and hands them to the suitors through the window. Odysseus spots the armed suitors, and Telemachus realizes that he himself left the door to the storeroom open. As Melanthius goes back to the storeroom for a second armload, Eumaeus catches sight of him and calls to Odysseus for instructions. Odysseus orders the swineherd and cattleman to overpower Melanthius, tie him to a plank, and hang the plank from the roof beams. They carry out their instructions and shut the storeroom door.

With 40 suitors left, Athena joins the 4 at the door in the guise of Mentor. Odysseus recognizes her, but the suitors do not, and Agelaus, who is now leading them, appeals to the man to join them. Athena responds by goading Odysseus to fight harder, but not yet giving any help in battle. She turns herself into a swallow and perches on a beam, but the suitors think Mentor has just departed. Agelaus urges the other 5 suitors with him to simultaneously attack Odysseus, believing that if Odysseus is killed, they can overcome the others without problem. They all heave their spears, but Athena protects Odysseus, and the return volley kills 4 more suitors. The suitors throw again, and again Athena turns the spears, but although Telemachus and Eumaeus receive superficial wounds, the return volley kills 4 more suitors including Ktesippos. Then Odysseus kills Agelaus, and Telemachus kills Leocritos, and the suitors are down to 30. Now Athena joins the battle with her aegis, and Leodes supplicates Odysseus, begging for mercy, but Odysseus kills him. Next Phemius, having carefully laid aside his harp, comes to Odysseus, clinging to his knees, and begs for mercy, saying he was compelled by the suitors. Telemachus seconds his claim, and adds that Medon the crier should also be spared. Hearing Telemachus' words, Medon comes out from under a chair where he was hidden wrapped in a bull's hide. Odysseus agrees and sends the 2 men outside. Turning to seek for any others living, he finds the men all dead like a catch of fish dumped on the beach.

Odysseus sends Telemachus to fetch Eurycleia. When she arrives in the hall and sees that her master's plan has succeeded and the house is free of the suitors, she is about to give a cry of triumph, but Odysseus stops her, saying that the will of the gods is responsible for the deaths, and it is not something to glory in. He asks her to identify the disloyal maids, and when she has, he has her send those 12 to him. He has them take the corpses to the courtyard and clean the tables and chairs, while Telemachus and the 2 servants clean the earthen floor. Then Telemachus and the servants take the disloyal maids out and hang them, and they mutilate and castrate Melanthius. The men go to wash, and Odysseus orders a brazier to be set in the hall to cleanse and purify it. When this is done, the servants come to greet Odysseus, embracing him and kissing his hands.

Book 22, cont.

# Book 23

## Journal and Discussion Topics

1. What first seems to convince Penelope that Eurycleia is telling the truth? Why do you think she finds this convincing?
2. What is Penelope's second thought to explain the death of the suitors without Odysseus' presence? Why do you think she changed her idea?
3. Why is Penelope so cautious?
4. What qualities does Odysseus exhibit in this book?
5. What deceptions occur in this book?
6. What if the *Odyssey* ended at the end of Book 23 when Odysseus sends Penelope to her room. Would it be a satisfying ending, or not? Explain.

## Summary

Eurycleia hurries up to Penelope's bedside and tells her that Odysseus has come home and has killed all the suitors. Penelope responds that this is the first time she has slept well since Odysseus went to war and now Eurycleia has disturbed her with false hopes. If Eurycleia were younger, Penelope would have her whipped out of the house. Eurycleia repeats her message, explaining that the stranger is Odysseus and that Telemachus has known for days. At this, Penelope jumps up and asks how he could fight all the suitors single-handed. Eurycleia tells her that she didn't see it, but only the corpses afterwards. Now they have cleansed the hall, and it is time to go down. Now Penelope has second thoughts, saying that a god has killed the suitors, but Odysseus is dead. Finally, Eurycleia tells her how she recognized the scar of the boar's tusk. Still believing that there is a god involved, not her husband, Penelope agrees to go down to greet her son, and see the dead and the stranger.

Entering the hall, her feelings in complete disarray, she sits by the near wall and gazes across the room at the man who sits leaning against a pillar. Telemachus upbraids her for her coldness. She responds that she is in shock, but that if this man is truly Odysseus there are secrets by which they will know each other. At this, Odysseus smiles and tells Telemachus to let his mother take her time, adding that they are wanted men, having killed, not just one, but many citizens. Telemachus declares himself and the 2 servants ready to fight with his father. Odysseus advises that the 3 of them put on fresh clothes, have the women dress up, and have the harper play a dance tune and pretend there is a wedding going on to allay suspicion. They follow his instructions and no one guesses the reality.

In the meantime, Eurycleia bathes and anoints Odysseus, and Athena enhances his looks. He returns to his chair in the hall, and still Penelope is silent. Now, he too chides her, and bids Eurycleia make a bed for him. Penelope begins to speak of how Odysseus looked when he left for Troy, but breaks off and bids Eurycleia to have the bed he built removed from the bedchamber, placed outside the room, and piled with covers. At this Odysseus is angered, asking how the bed, built with a living olive tree as part of its frame—their secret sign—could be moved. Penelope, convinced at last, runs to him, explaining that with all the deceptions that gods and men practice, coming as impostors, she had to be sure of his identity, and they weep in each other's arms. Athena slows down the night, and in the long wait for dawn, Odysseus tells Penelope of the journey Tiresias told him he must take, she tells him how she was courted by the suitors, and he tells her of his wanderings, and then they sleep.

In the morning, Odysseus tells Penelope that he will replace what he lost to the suitors from gifts given by friends and by going on raids. However, he first must visit his father, and—knowing that word of the suitors' deaths will soon be about—he tells Penelope to stay in her room with the women. Then he wakes Telemachus, Eumaeus, and Philoetius, and they arm and leave the town.

Book 23, cont.

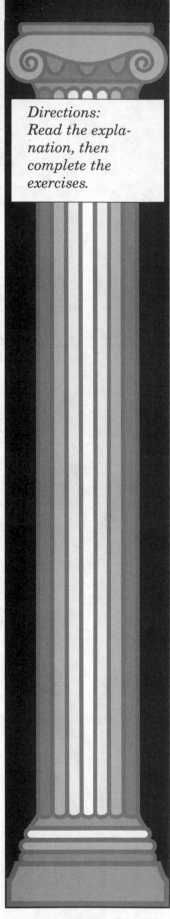

# STRATEGY 17 Character Traits

Directions:
Read the expla-
nation, then
complete the
exercises.

We often speak of **character traits** as absolutes—that is, characters either have them or not. So we might describe a character as resourceful and cunning. This is useful for a start. But even a character that we recognize as resourceful and cunning in general may be more or less cunning and more or less resourceful, depending on the situation. Considering the variations in character traits can be the first step in taking a more realistic view of the complex thing we call character. We can consider character traits as existing on a continuum, a scale with opposite traits at the ends and a whole range of possible points in between. For example:

hospitable——————————————————————inhospitable

Think about Alcinous: he is presented initially as a man who is especially dedicated to hospitality. In fact, as he listens to Odysseus, and comes to understand his character and situation, he becomes more and more hospitable. Now, think about the end of Book 13 when Alcinous responds to the turning of his ship to stone by Poseidon, fulfilling the prophecy. You can see that Alcinous' trait is responsive to circumstances and that to say that Alcinous is or isn't hospitable would not come near to telling the whole story.

1. For each continuum, write a paragraph telling how the character(s) indicated move(s) along it during the course of the book.

   patient——————————impatient
   (Penelope, Odysseus)

   uncertain——————confident
   (Telemachus, Penelope)

   honest————————deceptive
   (Odysseus, Athena)

   responsible—————-irresponsible
   (Odysseus)

2. Choose a single character and write a full-page description of his or her character traits. Explain how his or her behavior varies along each continuum that you identify.

# Book 24

## Journal and Discussion Topics

1. Analyze the accuracy of Amphimedon's retelling.
2. Why do you think Odysseus chose to test Laertes rather than run to him?
3. Why does Odysseus make up another new story to tell Laertes?
4. What do the Ithacans who are persuaded to take a side find to be convincing evidence?
5. Do you find the end of the *Odyssey* satisfying?  Why or why not?

## Summary

Hermes calls the ghosts of the suitors so he can lead them to the underworld. On the way, they meet the ghosts of Achilles, Patroclus, Antilochus, Ajax, and finally Agamemnon.  Achilles greets Agamemnon, empathizing with him over having an ignominious death at home, rather than a glorious death on the field of battle.  Agamemnon then recounts the aftermath of Achilles' death in battle: how the Achaeans and Trojans fought over his body; how the soldiers mourned him; how his mother Thetis and the nereids came mourning from the sea, and the Muses sang for him; how his funeral pyre was built, and his bones set in a golden amphora; and how the funeral games were held for him. Agamemnon says he cannot enjoy his victory in battle, since he came home to death.

Then Agamemnon, seeing his friend Amphimedon among the dead following Hermes, questions him about how so many men and so young came to die all at once. Amphimedon tells Agamemnon how the suitors came to the house after Odysseus had been long absent; how Penelope tried to evade marriage with the trick of the loom (and in some of the translations, how she wished for the suitors' deaths); how Odysseus came to Eumaeus' hut, and with Telemachus, planned the deaths of the suitors; how Telemachus came down to town first, and Odysseus followed in the guise of a beggar led by Eumaeus; how the suitors mistreated the beggar; how Zeus told Telemachus to move the arms to the storeroom and lock it, and Odysseus told Penelope to have the contest of the bow (these details differ from the tale Homer has told); how no one could string the bow and how they tried to keep the beggar from getting it, but Telemachus insisted (it doesn't mention here that Penelope also insisted); how the beggar strung the bow, shot an arrow through the axeheads, and began the killing by shooting Antinous; and how the beggar was eventually joined in battle by a god (he doesn't mention Telemachus and the 2 herdsmen) until all the suitors were dead.  He points out that their bodies lie still unburied in Odysseus' house. Agamemnon responds with joy that Odysseus has escaped the fate he himself suffered, because Penelope is a true wife.

In the meantime, Odysseus and his men reach Laertes' land.  Leaving his companions with instructions to prepare the noon meal, Odysseus goes to find his father, to try him, as he says.  When Odysseus finds him, Laertes is digging around a fruit tree, dressed in rags, and bowed with pain.  Odysseus stops and weeps, wondering if he should run to his father or test him, and decides on the

latter. He approaches his father, praising the trees, but suggesting that the man is less well cared for than the trees are, pretending to mistake him for a servant. Odysseus claims he once met a man from Ithaca whose father was named Laertes, and they became good friends, and he gave him many presents. Laertes gets tears in his eyes and tells the stranger that he's come to the right place, but the man of whom he speaks is not here to return his gifts and offer him hospitality in return, for he died far from home. Laertes asks the stranger for his story, and Odysseus responds with another made-up story, until Laertes scoops up dirt from the ground and pours it into his hair, groaning with grief. Finally, Odysseus embraces him, and announces his return and his revenge on the suitors. Laertes asks him for a sign, and Odysseus both shows him the scar from the boar's tusk and also names the fruit trees that Laertes gave him when he was a boy.

When Laertes recovers from the shock of recognition, he begins to worry about the outcry that is sure to follow the suitors' deaths. Odysseus tells him not to worry, and they go to join Telemachus and the herdsmen for their meal. The housekeeper bathes Laertes, and Athena makes him seem young again. Then Laertes' servants come in and are overjoyed to see Odysseus, and they all eat together.

Meanwhile, news of the suitors' deaths has gone around town, and people begin to collect the bodies, to bury them or ship them home. The men gather in assembly, and Antinous' father, Eupithes, speaks first, urging the assembly to quickly follow and capture Odysseus, and the crowd is moved by his tears for his son. But then Medon and Phemius arrive and Medon says that it was not only Odysseus who fought, but a god with him in the guise of Mentor, and this announcement makes the assembly fearful. Then Halitherses speaks, telling the Ithacans that the responsibility for these men's deaths rests with themselves—they did not heed his warnings, nor Mentor's, nor control their sons. He urges them to do nothing, to have this be the end of the matter. Many agree with Halitherses, but many also agree with Eupithes and go to arm themselves.

At the same time, Athena questions Zeus about his will, and he puts the matter into her hands to complete as she will, only suggesting that Odysseus should be made king forever and declaring that the guilt for the slaying shall be wiped out. Athena goes and enters the room where Odysseus and the others are finishing lunch, again in the shape of Mentor, just as the armed Ithacans are approaching. Athena tells Laertes to pray to herself and Zeus and throw his spear. He does, bringing down Eupithes, but just as the battle is about to be joined, Athena/Mentor shouts, stopping all in their tracks. She commands them to make peace. They drop their swords, and the men from town start to run away. Unaccountably, Odysseus makes to follow them, when Zeus sends down a thunderbolt. Athena tells Odysseus to stop and call off the battle, lest he anger Zeus. Odysseus obeys, and both sides swear to keep peace on the terms set by Athena/Mentor.

# Writer's Forum

## Compare and Contrast a Book and a Movie

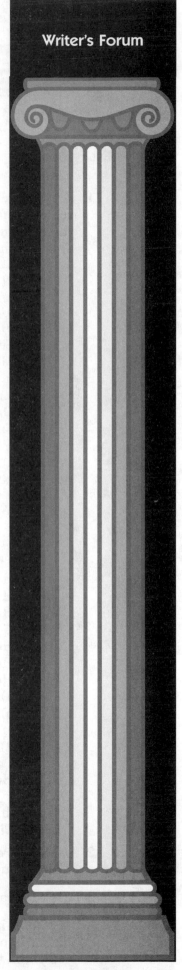

As you may recall from the Writer's Forum on a compare and contrast essay (page 50), in such an essay you show the similarities and differences between 2 or more people, things, ideas, approaches, etc., and draw some conclusion(s) based on this examination. You choose the categories to compare and contrast based on your purpose, and these categories will change depending on your topic.

Sometimes, when considering literature, you will want to compare and contrast 2 different treatments of the same subject in different versions, genres, or media. You might want to do this if a work has been adapted or translated to create a new work, or if a work has inspired or influenced another work, or if they have the same subject and enough in common or such wide differences that you think it would be fruitful to see the similarities and differences in how they make meaning and achieve their effects.

In this particular case, you are going to contrast the book of the *Odyssey* with the movie made from the book. Usually it is easier to do this if you both read the book twice and watch the movie at least twice, once to experience it, and once to take notes for your paper. Here are some questions that it would be useful to examine:

- A movie is usually no longer than 2 hours, so a movie adaptation of a book leaves out material included in the book. What is excerpted or compressed in this movie?
- A movie script may have additional material not included in the book, or may make changes in the book. What additions and/or changes do you notice?
- How did your mental images of the characters, settings, and actions of the book differ from the way they were presented in the movie? Compare the characterizations and the plots carefully.
- Apart from the book, did the movie work as an experience in itself? Did it hold your interest? Was it worthwhile?
- Did the theme(s) you identified in the book come out in the movie? If not, what message(s) did the movie give?
- Which did you like better—the book or the movie? Why?

Source words that can help you express concepts of similarity and difference include the following:

- as well as
- similarly
- differ
- whereas
- however
- likewise
- alike
- while
- but
- on the contrary
- at the same time
- resemble
- conversely
- though
- on the other hand

1. Write an essay comparing and contrasting the book and the movie of the *Odyssey*.

**Essay Topics**

1. Barry B. Powell in his study, "Composition by Theme in the *Odyssey*" (1977), gives a schema that he believes helps capture the basic elements that Homer uses repeatedly in the episodes of Odysseus' adventures. Study the schema and apply it to 3 of the following episodes, including the suitors as one of your choices:

   a. Calypso      b. Polyphemus      c. Aeolus      d. Circe      e. the Suitors

   - I.      a) Stops on an island
            b) After a storm
   - II.     Sees smoke
   - III.    Meets and 'tries' a benevolent figure
        The figure is:   a) motherly
                         b) potential wife
   - IV.    Or meets and 'tries' a demonic figure
        The figure is:   a) ignorant of human arts, boorish
                         b) of odd shape, large size
                         c) gluttonous, marauder
                         d) cave-dweller
                         e) earth, water, underworld
                         f) wind, storm, mist
                         g) free from want, strife
                         h) unconsciousness, sleep
   - V.      There is a sacrifice, banquet
   - VI.     Hero is overcome
   - VII.    He has been betrayed
   - VIII.   He overcomes an enemy:   a) through trickery
                                      b) through strength
   - IX.     He has a special weapon or magical object
   - X.      He has a helper
   - XI.     He is recognized
            a) by an object
            b) by a story
            c) by a change of state
            d) by a feat of cunning; or strength
   - XII.    Prophecy has been fulfilled
   - XIII.   He is purified
   - XIV.    a) He gets the girl
            b) or receives a treasure
   - XV.     The victory is celebrated

2. If you were asked to classify the *Odyssey* as primarily an adventure story or a love story, which would you call it and why?

3. Looking back, what was your favorite part of the story, and why?

4. Try to think of some new understanding that you gained from reading the *Odyssey*. Either explain what it was and what it means to you, or—if you had none—explain why you think this story didn't enrich your understanding.

## Strategy 1: Genre — Epic, page 11

1. Answers will vary depending on the translation the student is using. Students may note that lines have a regular number of beats.
2. Answers will vary depending on the translation the student is using. Possible answers: gray-eyed goddess (Athena); O swineherd Eumaeus; much-enduring, great Odysseus.
3. Answers will vary depending on the translation the student is using. Possible responses: "slung a sharp sword over his shoulder," Lattimore II, 3; Rouse II, second sentence; "over his shoulder he slung his well-honed sword," Fagles II, 3; "slung on a sword-belt and a new-edged sword," Fitzgerald II, 4.
4. Answers will vary. Students may discuss sharing information with others so that it will be recalled or using memorizing techniques; having a very different system of education and a differently organized body of knowledge about the world.

## Strategy 2: Translations, pages 12–14

1. A, B, D, E, and G all seem fairly similar and therefore can be identified as translations. C is in a different genre and therefore must be an adaptation. The narrator of F has clearly reorganized the information and this is a retelling of the story.
2. Answers will vary. Students should support their choice with reasons.
3. The archaic syntax and spelling identify A as the early translation.
4. Answers will vary. Possible responses: B is prose and rendered more loosely, while the others are poetry and seem to be nearly line-for-line. E uses alliteration and consonance more than the others. B calls the Sun god "Hyperion," while D and E refer to him as "Helios."

## Strategy 3: Background—The Historical Troy, pages 15–16

1. The site matches Troy for historical period, bears out geographical statements from the *Iliad* and the tradition of later authors, and includes artifacts (like the helmet) that closely match Homer's descriptions. Moreover, there is no alternative site in the vicinity.
2. Timelines should reflect the events mentioned and be proportioned to appropriately represent the passage of time.

## Strategy 4: Homer's Mythology, pages 17–18

1. Students may find conflicting information on all 4 questions mentioned — the number of Sirens, Scylla's parentage, the name of Oedipus' mother, the source of the idea to use the Trojan horse to enter the city — as well as in other areas.

## Strategy 5: Beginning a Book, pages 19–20

1. Students may not have much reaction to the title if they have never heard of Odysseus. If they have seen the movie or read other works that refer to him, they may have some reaction.
2. Answers will vary depending on the translation the student is using.
3. Answers will vary depending on the translation the student is using.
4. Answers will vary.
5. Answers will vary depending on the translation the student is using. Students will have a much fuller idea from Lattimore's glosses on the books or from Rouse's book titles (if they flip through and read them) than from Fitzgerald's or Fagles's book titles, from which they may only be able to glean that this is an adventure story.
6. An unidentified man is the protagonist and the god Poseidon is an antagonist.
7. Students should realize that the story takes place in the ancient Greek world in a setting with real and imaginary elements. They should note the role of the gods in human affairs, the magical elements, and the focus on Odysseus' house and the events there.
8. Students should note the focus on Odysseus' homecoming, but they may also note the attention paid to order/disorder, hospitality, recognition/disguise, and achieving manhood.
9. Answers will vary. Students may predict that Athena will do more to make Odysseus' homecoming possible and Telemachus will set out to look for his father.
10. Answers will vary.

## Introduction to Fagles's *Odyssey*, pages 21–22

**Introduction**

1a. There is a continuous history of the text being in print back to 1488, and handwritten copies in Italy for about 100 years prior to that. For the thousand years before that, it was kept alive in Byzantium in manuscript books printed on vellum or paper and before that on parchment. In the ancient world, it was transmitted on 24 papyrus scrolls and can be traced back to the sixth century B.C.

1b. The *Odyssey* was composed by an epic poet working in the oral, improvisational tradition.

1c. The answer is not clear. Recent scholars believe that writing may have played a part in the composition of the *Odyssey* and that Homer himself may have written it down.

2. The *Odyssey* was composed after the *Iliad* by a poet who knew the *Iliad* well and avoided repeating details from it. Characterization is consistent in the two poems.

3. To return home.

4. The theme is hospitality—the relationship of hosts and guests and the moral responsibility people have for the stranger who comes among them. Every episode is a variation on this theme.

5. Their attitude toward deception.

6. Their choice to follow Zeus' code and help the stranger, Odysseus, return home leads to their inability to ever help another stranger return home over the sea.

7. He characterizes it as harsh and links it to adolescent rebellion against his mother, aggravated by the absence of his father.

8. He suggests that she suspected that none of them would succeed in stringing the bow, freeing her from their unwanted attentions for good.

9. He lists the unfinished plot elements that remain to be settled—the consequences of the slaughter of the suitors in the community of Ithaca, the meeting between Odysseus and Laertes, and the fulfillment of Theoclymenus' prophecy about the suitors descent into the realm of death.

**Homeric Geography**

1. The second map shows a view farther south than the first map. The third map goes even farther south as well as farther east than the second.

2. It is the unlabeled island in the upper left-hand corner, just northeast of Same.

3. Somewhere about 525 miles, depending on the route.

**Translator's Postscript**

1. He uses "virtual repetition" in longer passages, but tries to give the nuance of the context to capture the spirit of the epithets.

2. He is influenced by his fundamental commitment to a 5- or 6-beat line, as well as the meaning of the particular line, the need for emphasis, and the cadence of the English words.

3. He was helped by his collaborator Bernard Knox, who commented on his drafts and wrote the Introduction and Notes; by earlier translators, friends, and fellow classicists; by his university, which gave him time off, and by his editors and other publishing staff; and finally by his daughters and his wife.

4. Odysseus' journey continues both because we know that he must make the prescribed trip to appease Poseidon and because Odysseus is reincarnated, so to speak, in the adventures of Aeneas, Ulysses, Adam, Bloom, and other literary figures who follow in his footsteps.

**The Genealogies**

1. Zeus is his great-grandfather.

2. Great-grandfather and great-uncle.

3. They are uncle and niece as well as husband and wife.

4. He is Nausicaa's great-grandfather on her father's side and her great-great-grandfather on her mother's side. He is Nestor's grandfather.

## Introduction to Fitzgerald's *Odyssey,* page 23

**Postscript**

1. He concludes that Homer also made mistakes.

2. He tries to find a reading that makes syntactical and verbal sense and is appropriately dramatic to the context.

3. He imagines that there are holes in the axeheads, that they are used alone without helves, and that they are pressed into the earth dug up from the trench. He also considers that Odysseus held the bow horizontally.

4. Students' sketches should be based on pages 478–481.
5. Although the word is usually translated "vulture," Homer uses a different word for vulture and this clearly indicates a hunting bird not a carrion bird. There is also a different word for eagle that Homer uses. In addition, another translator, John Moore, translates the word as "falcon" in the *Ajax*.
6. He says it could have been composed by a single "singer" considering that the medium (oral epic) and themes had already been developed by others—he therefore considers it both as a collaborative work and the work of a single author.
7. He imagines the performer as a combination of actor, singer, poet, and harp player all rolled into one.
8. Students may follow Fitzgerald's division or suggest an alternative.
9. They come from the same collection of stories; they were composed in the same tradition, although the *Odyssey* was composed second; in places, the *Odyssey* parodies the *Iliad,* but does not repeat it.
10. He suggests that although she may not consciously know it, the prophecy and Odysseus' presence, even in the guise of a beggar, is in some way known to Penelope, and explains otherwise inexplicable actions (why does she justify her treatment of the suitors and explain herself to a beggar?). He further shows how Penelope completes the plan of conquering the suitors that Odysseus had left unfinished by creating the test of the bow, and asks (in effect), how can we believe, with both the diviner's prophecy and the beggar's promise that her husband would be with her the following day, that she could not wait to see if the promises were true and decided to pick a husband the following day?
11. He bases his claim both on the earlier references to Laertes that must be tied up, as well as the playing out of the consequences of the deaths of the suitors and the winding up of the theme of comparison between the homecoming of Agamemnon and that of Odysseus.
12. Students' understanding of this theme will vary.

## Introduction to Lattimore's *Odyssey,* page 24

1. Answers will vary. Students may agree that it is useful to have terms to work with without necessarily agreeing with Lattimore's divisions. They may comment on the creation of a section that includes Books v–viii and part of xiii, but not ix–xii.
2. Answers will vary. Students may suggest that the order might be chronological, rather than following first Odysseus (the first paragraph) and then going back to his family. They may point out that omission of any mention of Odysseus' being in disguise (as opposed to simply "unrecognized") makes the summary less clear than it might be.
3. The respect that Nestor, Menelaus, and Athena show for Odysseus in the Telemachy increases Odysseus' importance in the audience's mind; it allows for references to Troy and introduction of well-known characters that couldn't otherwise have been worked into the storyline; it creates a justifiable reason for the eventual murder of the suitors; it establishes Athena's role as Odysseus' protector and stage manager of the drama; and it establishes Telemachus as having the character to act in the role of his father's helper.
4. As part of the greater story of the homecoming of the Achaeans from Troy; as the wanderings that Odysseus himself recounts between Troy and Calypso's island; as the continuation home from Calypso's island; and the false stories of wanderings that Odysseus tells when he is in disguise.
5. He believes they are combinations of real and imaginary places.
6. He says that symbolism is not characteristic of early Greek epic, that the particularity of the adventures shows that they are meant to portray a unique man, not the human race,
7. Students may or may not agree that the slowed-down action allows some interesting literary effects.
8. Students may or may not agree that the doom of the suitors is excessive. Some students may think that at least Amphinomus should have been spared.
9. It disposes of the suitor's bodies, reconnects the story to the Trojan War, provides the promised reunion with Laertes, and gives the necessary reconciliation of the families of the dead suitors with their ruler.
10. They both ignore historical developments; the *Odyssey* assumes the existence of the *Iliad;* the main characters are "the same people" in both; all material mentioned in the *Iliad* is carefully excluded from the *Odyssey*.

## Introduction to Rouse's *Odyssey*, page 25
### "On First Looking into Chapman's Homer"
1. Answers will vary. Students should have the idea that Chapman's translation of Homer gave the speaker (Keats, himself?) a vision and sense of discovery that he likens to that of the great explorers and that he had not previously experienced, even when he himself traveled and explored.
2. Possible response: It is a metonymy—from the speaker's description of Homer's forehead as "deep," we are to conclude that the thoughts inside his head were also "deep" (container for the thing contained).
3. It was Balboa, not Cortez (Cortés), who was the first European to see the Pacific Ocean.
4. Answers will vary.

### Preface
1. The language used is affected and attempts to be poetic, which only makes it sound unnatural.
2. He claims to speak naturally, as Homer does.

### Homer's Words
1. Possible response: Literary style is art, relying on rhetoric, wit, and educated language rather than on feeling, humor, and the natural language of speech.
2a. Possible response: The forms reflected common speech.
2b. Possible response: The words are natural with no attempts at creating an artificial "poetic" language.
2c. Possible response: They are traditional without being clichéd.
3. Possible response: Homer's language is colloquial, and he uses commonplace and simple words.

## Book 1, pages 26–27
Answers will vary. Allow for individual opinion.
1. Students should recognize both the power of Zeus and rule by the will of the majority that Zeus expresses when he talks about Poseidon being one against the many.
2. Students should note that the gods can both determine the future of mortals, and also (like Athena) interact with humans, appearing in human form, or in other forms. They should see, however, that Athena uses persuasion and advice with Telemachus, and in this way respects his will.
3. Answers will vary. It can be interpreted as questioning Penelope's veracity, or simply as bitterness over the loss of the father he never really knew.
4. Possible response: His father is absent, so the household is unprotected. He does not know if his father is dead or alive, so he cannot tell what to do about another marriage for his mother. The suitors are occupying his house and despoiling his estate, but he is too young and powerless to stand up to them. He seems to have no older man to advise him (until Athena comes along as Mentes).
5. She advises him to call an assembly and ask the suitors to leave the house. Then, he should visit Nestor and Menelaus to try to find news of Odysseus, and either wait for his return if he is alive, or, if he is dead, hold his funeral and give Penelope in marriage to another man.
6. Orestes.
7. Answers will vary. Students' responses may partly depend on which translation they are reading. They may find Telemachus harsh, despite the comment that Penelope recognized the wisdom of what he said. They may take this as a sign of Telemachus' empowerment after the encouragement of Athena.
8. Answers will vary. Students may say that in Telemachus' situation, they would follow Athena's advice, and in Penelope's they would try another trick to delay the suitors.
9. Answers will vary.
10. Answers will vary.
11. Students predictions should be grounded in the details of the chapter, particularly the statements about the future made by the speaker, Zeus, and Athena.
12. Students may compare the poet to an actor, or feel that in some way the speaker's and poet's voices are melded.

## Strategy 6: Plot—Beginning/Middle/End, pages 28–29
Students need to read beyond Book 1 (and, in some cases, complete the story) in order to answer these questions.
1. Answers will vary. Students' descriptions should accurately reflect the organization of the story.
2. Answers will vary. Students should recognize that the material in Books 5–12 occurs prior to the material presented in Books 1–4.

3. Answers will vary. Students may say that the tale would be easier to follow or that the tale would hold together better because the focus wouldn't shift from Odysseus to Telemachus back to Odysseus. Students may cite as gains the points that Lattimore makes about the effectiveness of the Telemachy: The respect that Nestor, Menelaus, and Athena show for Odysseus in the Telemachy increases Odysseus' importance in the audience's mind; the Telemachy allows for references to Troy and introduction of well-known characters that couldn't otherwise have been worked into the storyline; it creates a justifiable reason for the eventual murder of the suitors; it establishes Athena's role as Odysseus' protector and stage manager of the drama; and it establishes Telemachus as having the character to act in the role of his father's helper.

4. Answers will vary. The background of Odysseus' scar is perhaps the best-known instance.

5. Answers will vary. There are repetitions of sacrifices, false stories told by Odysseus, revelations of Odysseus' true identity, etc. There are parallels between Agamemnon's family and situation and Odysseus' family and situation, etc.

6. Answers will vary. Some critics consider the background on Odysseus' scar coming when it does was inserted as a technique to delay the telling of Eurycleia's reaction and to add interest to the narrative.

## Strategy 7: References and Allusions, page 30

1. The mentions of Agamemnon and his family are (line numbers from Fitzgerald)

| Book | Lines | Speaker | Notes |
|---|---|---|---|
| 1 | 45–62 | Zeus | Reference (explicit); contrast between Aegisthus and Odysseus; relationship of gods and people |
| 1 | 345–348 | Athena | Reference (explicit); parallel between Orestes and Telemachus; inspire Telemachus to act |
| 3 | 209–214 | Nestor | Reference (explicit); parallel between Orestes and Telemachus; praise of Telemachus |
| 3 | 250–253 | Athena | Reference (explicit); contrast between Agamemnon's homecoming and Odysseus'; Odysseus' sufferings are preferable to his death. |
| 3 | 267–339 | Telemachus/Nestor | Reference (explicit); contrast between Agamemnon's known death and Odysseus' unknown death (in Telemachus' mind); Nestor is answering a direct question that Telemachus asked. |
| 4 | 98–99 | Menelaus | Students may identify this as either a reference (because Menelaus says "my brother") or an allusion (because none of the people involved are named); contrast between Menelaus' homecoming and Agamemnon's; what Menelaus feels was lost on account of the Trojan War. |
| 4 | 547–583 | Proteus/Menelaus | Reference (explicit); contrast between the fate of Menelaus' two companions; Proteus is answering Menelaus' question |
| 11 | 451–534 | Odysseus/dead Agamemnon | Reference (explicit); Agamemnon claims a parallel between Clytemnestra and Penelope, but Homer is pointing to a contrast between the two women; Odysseus asks Agamemnon how he died. |
| 13 | 480–485 | Odysseus | Reference (explicit); Odysseus compares what would have happened to him without Athena's intercession with Agamemnon's fate; Odysseus is using the analogy to show his understanding of his situation. |
| 24 | 109–111 | dead Agamemnon | Reference (explicit); Homer is (again) comparing Clytemnestra and Penelope; Agamemnon is filling Achilles in on what happened after he died. |
| 24 | 216–228 | dead Agamemnon | Reference (explicit); Agamemnon is contrasting Odysseus' homecoming with his own; Agamemnon is reacting to Amphimedon's story of the death of the suitors. |

## Book 2, pages 31–32

Answers will vary. Allow for individual opinion.

1. Students should note that the Council has not met for 20 years, and this makes it seem that it functions primarily in relation to the king. Since Telemachus asks them for a ship and crew, it seems that they have some power, but the extent of it is not clear.
2. Students may say that the responsibility lies with the suitors, Penelope, Telemachus, the community of Ithaca, or some combination of these. They should support their opinion with reasons.
3. Students' reactions may or may not be sympathetic. Possible response: The crowd's reaction might indicate that it was acceptable for men to cry, and that it wasn't considered inappropriate to express strong feelings in public.
4. Answers will vary. Students may propose that Telemachus ask her real feelings, or they may feel that such a straightforward approach would be too uncomfortable between a mother and son.
5. Answers will vary. Possible responses:
   Telemachus—passionately, but fairly
   Eurymachus—rudely and selfishly
   Halitherses—responsibly and warningly
   Antinous—rudely and unfeelingly
   Mentor—eloquently and ironically
6. Leocritus has the last word, and he seems to indicate that the Council as a whole will not act—those who individually support Telemachus may help him on their own account.
7. Students should mention Penelope's trickery in weaving and secretly unweaving the shroud, Athena's appearing as Mentor and Telemachus, and Telemachus' insistence that Eurycleia deceive Penelope about his whereabouts.
8. She mentions how much he is loved by those at home, that the suitors will plot to kill him and divide his inheritance, and the hardships of life at sea.
9. She secures a ship and crew for Telemachus, sails with him on his voyage, and provides a wind.
10. Answers will vary. Students may predict that they will plot to kill Telemachus, or attempt to secure Penelope's hand while he's gone.

## Strategy 8: Setting—Real and Imaginary Places, page 33

Page numbers and descriptions will vary with the translation used. The following information will guide you.

| Book | Setting Name(s) |
|---|---|
| 1 | Olympus; Ithaca |
| 2 | Ithaca |
| 3 | Pylos |
| 4 | Sparta; Ithaca |
| 5 | Olympus; Calypso's island; at sea, Scheria |
| 6 | Scheria |
| 7 | Scheria |
| 8 | Scheria |
| 9 | (For books 9–12, Odysseus is in Scheria, but telling the story of his wanderings elsewhere); land of the Cicones; land of the Lotus-Eaters; land of the Cyclops |
| 10 | (Scheria) land of Aeolus; in sight of Ithaca; land of Aeolus; land of the Laistrygonians; Circe's island |
| 11 | (Scheria) Land of the Dead; Scheria; Circe's island |
| 12 | (Scheria) Sirens; Scylla and Charybdis; Helios' island; Calypso's island; Scheria |
| 13 | Ithaca |
| 14 | Ithaca |
| 15 | Ithaca |
| 16 | Ithaca |
| 17 | Ithaca |
| 18 | Ithaca |
| 19 | Ithaca |
| 20 | Ithaca |
| 21 | Ithaca |

| | |
|---|---|
| **22** | Ithaca |
| **23** | Ithaca |
| **24** | Ithaca |

## Book 3, page 34

Answers will vary. Allow for individual opinion.
1. Students should note that he uses the sun's movement in the sky to tell time. As evidence, they might note the following (or examples from other Books): Homer opens both Book 2 and Book 3 with the sunrise; he speaks of the sun going down while Nestor speaks, the sun rising just before Nestor leaves his room, the sun being low in the sky when Telemachus and Pisistratus reach Pherai, the sun going down as Book 3 ends.
2. Students should note the line that indicates that Athena herself answered or helped to answer the prayers that she made to Poseidon; however, their opinions about what this indicates may differ. There does seem to be some rivalry between the 2 and definite difference of opinion about Odysseus.
3. Students should mention the courtesy due to a guest (Telemachus and Athena/Mentes in Book 1; Nestor's family and Telemachus and Athena/Mentor in Book 3)—guests are not questioned until after they have eaten; offering guests a bath seems to be in order; an exchange of gifts between host and guest seems to be customary.
4. They foolishly called an assembly when night was falling and the soldiers were drunk, and then argued in front of the troops, creating a division of opinion in the army that then split into 2 factions.
5. The suitors will use up or steal his property.
6. They offer sacrifices and prayers to the gods.
7. Possible response: because honoring the gods is so important in this society. Students may note a contrast with the suitors, who do not offer a sacrifice before they eat in Book 1 and whose comments to Halitherses (Book 2) and behavior show disdain for the gods.

## Book 4, page 35

Answers will vary. Allow for individual opinion.
1. Possible response: his suggestion that they send the strangers away violates the code of hospitality, which is part of what allowed Menelaus to return home from Troy.
2. Possible response: Odysseus was the man most dear to Menelaus, the one whom he most admired and misses the most.
3. Helen and Menelaus conceal their recognition of Telemachus; Helen drugs the wine; Odysseus disguised himself as a beggar and entered Troy; the Achaeans hid in the wooden horse; Helen imitated the voices of the Achaeans' wives to try to trick them into leaving the horse; Menelaus and his 3 men disguised themselves as seals; Proteus changed his shape; Aegisthus deceived Agamemnon, leading him to a feast and murdering him; Telemachus and Athena deceive the suitors, leaving Ithaca in spite of them; Telemachus deceives Penelope, leaving Ithaca without telling her; Eurycleia also deceives Penelope by provisioning Telemachus without telling her; Athena makes Penelope believe that her sister had come to her in a dream; the suitors set an ambush for Telemachus.
4. Menelaus lays the responsibility for Helen's actions not with Helen, but with some deity. Students may think that he is just trying to save face, or that, given what Helen said in the speech just prior, that he has found the true reason for her seemingly contradictory behavior.
5. Students' pictures should reflect Menelaus' tenacity and Proteus' changing shape.
6. He praises Menelaus' hospitality, while explaining that to stay would be difficult for his shipmates; he praises the horses and the land of Sparta, while explaining that Ithaca is not a good place for horses to live.
7. Antinous is angry because Telemachus defied the suitors and actually went to Pylos. He plans to ambush and murder Telemachus before he returns to Ithaca.
8. Possible response: because Telemachus does not have the training to stand up to the hardships of the world.
9. Athena sends Penelope a dream to reveal to her that Athena is caring for Telemachus and protecting him.

## Test 1: Books 1–4, page 36

1. Possible responses: Since most of the characters either really do or really don't want Odysseus to come home, our attention is focused on Odysseus even though he's not present. The main plot action is Telemachus' search for news of Odysseus. Many of the stories told and discussion are about Odysseus—from the servants in Ithaca to the gods on Olympus, Odysseus makes up part of their conversation. The part that is not about Telemachus' search takes place on the island of which Odysseus was (is) ruler, and in his house.
2. Answers will vary. Students may mention that Athena has more of a role in the plot in Books 1–4; she is present more and is more effective. Penelope is important in that she motivates the action of the suitors both in their staying at Odysseus' house and in their planning to kill Telemachus.
3. Answers will vary. Students' opinions may reflect their judgment about her responsibility for the Trojan War.
4. Possible response: At the end of Book 4, he seems more mature and independent, and more like a partner to Athena than a tag-along.
5. Answers will vary. Students may mention hospitality to strangers, homecoming, community, maturity.
6. Answers will vary. Students' predictions should be based on evidence from the text.
7. Answers will vary depending on the story picked. Possible responses include *Danny, Champion of the World*; *Death of a Salesman;* the Biblical story of Abraham and Isaac; *Cheaper by the Dozen; The Way of All Flesh.*
8. Answers will vary depending on the story picked. Possible responses include *The Hobbit, Redwall, Treasure Island, Over Sea and Under Stone, Blue Highways, Watership Down.*
9. Answers will vary. Students should support their answers with reasons.

## Book 5, page 37

Answers will vary. Allow for individual opinion.
1. Some of the speech is identical in the Greek, but answers will vary depending on the translation students are using. Lattimore and Fagles render the lines exactly the same way. Fitzgerald renders them nearly identically. Rouse's versions are very dissimilar in their wording. Answers will vary. It could be showing the close affinity between Athena and the man she pretended to be. It could be showing how wise Mentor is, because it shows that his estimation of Odysseus is like Athena's. It could be indicating that Athena put that speech in Mentor's mind. It could be showing that the poet needed a speech in praise of Odysseus as ruler, and since he already had one ready-made, he used it.
2. Answers will vary. Possible response: To reset the stage for the reader to the focus on Odysseus that began Book 1.
3. It is rendered in rhymed couplets.
4. The gods are jealous because she has taken a mortal as her lover.
5. The way Calypso presents her decision to let Odysseus go is a deception, since she takes credit herself and does not mention the orders she received from Zeus.
6. Answers will vary. He forgoes immortality.
7. Students' summaries will vary. They should include the points mentioned in the chapter summary.

## Strategy 9: The Hero's Journey, page 38

I. Agamemnon refers briefly in Book 24 to the journey that he and Menelaus took to Ithaca to recruit Odysseus for the Trojan War.
II. This is not told in the *Odyssey.*
III. It is clear that Athena is the helper in Odysseus' journey, but the initiation of this role is not recounted.
IV. This is hard to pinpoint. Students may feel that the Lotus-Eaters—the first magical adventure upon leaving Troy—marks the beginning of the adventures in the realm of the unknown.
V. The visit to the Land of the Dead marks this part of the journey.
VI. The rest of the wanderings are the trials.
VII. This corresponds to Odysseus landing on Ithaca.
VIII. This transition occurs in Eumaeus' dwelling.
IX. This doesn't seem to be present.
X. This seems to come in Books 23–24.

## Writer's Forum: Persuasion, pages 39–40

1. Students' persuasive monologues should reflect the goal, the speaker, and the audience and use valid techniques for argument.

## Book 6, page 41

Answers will vary. Allow for individual opinion.

1. To help bring about Odysseus' homecoming.
2. Students may mention location (river vs. home or laundromat), equipment (rocks/beach vs. washing machine/dryer), cleaning agent (water only vs. soap/detergent); amount of time needed; travel; amount of exertion needed; frequency.
3. Nausicaa only stayed because Athena gave her courage. Running away was the natural reaction.
4. He praises her beauty and resemblance to the gods. He prays to the gods for her to have whatever her heart desires.
5. Because it is clear to her that Odysseus is trustworthy and because as a stranger and beggar he is under Zeus' protection so that they are obligated to help him.
6. Answers will vary. She may be letting him know that she finds him attractive. She may simply be warning him that his presence could be dangerous to her reputation and explaining to him implicitly that she is relying on his good manners and careful attention to her directions to protect her from gossip.
7. Out of deference to Poseidon.

## Strategy 10: Similes and Metaphors, page 42

1. A. implied metaphor followed by extended simile; B. extended simile; C. extended simile; D. extended simile.
2. Answers will vary. Students should note that: the doe/suitors are foolish to go into the lion's lair/Odysseus' house and powerless to oppose the owner's wrath when he finds them there; Odysseus and the spark are kept alive by being buried temporarily.
3. Answers will vary. Students may express a preference for one of each pair of translations or they may give a more analytic response.
4. The extended simile comparing the mountain lion and Odysseus can be found in Fagles, page 172; Fitzgerald, page 103; Lattimore, page 105; and Rouse, pages 75–76. Answers about meaning will vary. Students may either express personal feelings or give a more analytic response. Odysseus looks as dangerous as a mountain lion on the prowl.

## Book 7, page 43

Answers will vary. Allow for individual opinion.

1. Because she is a descendant of Poseidon and filled with grace and wisdom and fairness.
2. Students should mention at least some of the following: the height of the rooms, the precious metals and gems, the metalwork by Hephaestus, the fine embroidery, the number of maids, the amount of food, the large orchard and vegetable garden.
3. To celebrate a feast day in his honor and give him a safe trip home.
4. He blames himself for what appears to Alcinous to be a breach of manners.
5. He wonders if he is a god; he offers to make him his son-in-law and give him a home, land, and wealth in Scheria.

## Strategy 11: Characterization, page 44

1. He uses the words of Nausicaa, Athena, and Arete herself; the narrator's description of her appearance; her interaction with Odysseus; the symbolism of her name, which means "virtue" in Greek (most students will not know this); and the setting of her palace.
2. Possible responses: Telemachus thinks all night at the end of Book 1, Helen thinks of drugging the wine in Book 4, and in Book 6, Odysseus thinks about the best kind of speech to make to Nausicaa. Most characters' ideas are given as direct discourse. Possible response: action, even verbal action, is more interesting than unspoken thoughts to the audience.
3. Students should recognize that Odysseus has a wide range of interaction styles depending on the situation. He has appeared as a warrior, supplicant/beggar, reluctant lover, husband, guest, etc.

4. Answers will vary. Because Odysseus has appeared in so many different roles and in only 3 Books so far, students will not be able to definitively talk about character change after reading only Books 1–7.

5. While wording will vary, students should recognize that Athena is a guide/guard/helper/intercessor who has a certain amount of power, but not absolute power to help Odysseus, and who acts within a framework in which respect for other gods (Zeus and Poseidon) limits the range of her actions.

## Book 8, page 45

Answers will vary. Allow for individual opinion.

1. Athena disguises herself as Alcinous' crier and as the Phaeacian who measures Odysseus' discus throw. Students may or may not consider Athena's enhancement of Odysseus' appearance a deception.

2. Readers of Rouse, Fagles, and Fitzgerald will see the English meanings of the Greek names—all related to the sea. Lattimore just transliterates the Greek.

3. Odysseus says first to Laodamas that his thoughts are consumed by things other than athletic contests. In answer to Seareach/Broadsea/Euryalos, he says that you cannot judge people by appearances.

4. Possible response: Despite not even knowing Odysseus' name, he arranges his voyage home and creates a festival day for him. He generously commands all the princes of the realm (himself included) to bring gifts for Odysseus to take home. He is sensitive to Odysseus' reaction to the song, and arranges for Demodocus to cease. He then gently urges Odysseus to speak.

5. Answers will vary. Students may point out that the view of the gods doesn't seem to be consistent. In this Book alone, although Zeus is praised for having given prowess and skill to the Phaeacians and the gods are credited with giving people all their talents and gifts, they are also mocked through the story of Ares and Aphrodite tricking Hephaestus.

6. They have no steering mechanism—they read the minds of the crew and know where to go.

7. Answers will vary. Perhaps he sees it as a good segue into his revelation of his identity—a kind of preparation for his revelation. Maybe he is still irked by the incident with Seareach/Broadsea/Euryalos, and wants to hear praise of other accomplishments besides athletics.

8. He cites the rules of host/guest relationships and also suggests that Odysseus' behavior has aroused curiosity about his identity.

9. Answers will vary. Students may or may not feel that the gifts and speech were satisfactory. They should explain why they feel as they do.

## Test 2: Books 5–8, page 46

1. Answers will vary. Students may identify more with Telemachus because of his age and status, or more with Odysseus because he is the main focus of the story.

2. Answers will vary. Students should support their choice with reasons.

3. Students may suggest that he either will or won't identify himself. Students should note that in every other host/guest situation, the guest has answered the host's questions as soon as their first meal together was done. Odysseus has not followed this custom. Depending on the reason they assign, they may come to different conclusions. Possible response: Because the Phaeacians are related to Poseidon, Odysseus might have feared that they would not be friendly toward him. Therefore, he exacts the promise and sees all the preparations made for his homecoming before he reveals who he is.

4. Answers will vary depending on the element of Greek culture students choose and local practice in regard to that aspect of culture.

5. Students may find the Telemachy artistically useful or not. They should support their judgment with reasons.

6. Students may feel that the minor conflict adds interest to the story.

7. Students should note the parallel requests Athena makes to Zeus, followed by a god going to earth and carrying out a mission, and the parallel situations of son and father arriving unannounced at someone's house as a stranger, making claims on their hospitality.

8. Students should note the prediction that Alcinous mentions in his last speech of Book 8. Considering Poseidon's feelings about Odysseus, it would seem that this voyage may be in danger. It is, however, also true that Zeus has declared Odysseus' homecoming with certainty, so even if it is delayed or difficult, it will happen.

## Book 9, pages 47–48
Answers will vary. Allow for individual opinion.
1. Possible response: He makes a good decision at the land of the Cicones, although his crew doesn't follow it; he saves the men who ate the lotus flowers; he saves himself and some of his companions from being eaten by Polyphemus through his ingenuity.
2. Possible response: Attacking the Cicones in the first place, for no apparent reason; waiting to meet Polyphemus instead of leaving or stealing the sheep and leaving, because his curiosity resulted in the death of some of his men; telling Polyphemus his name, because his bragging leads to Polyphemus' prayer which leads to the death of all his men. (Until they have read Book 7, students will not know that all Odysseus' men do, in fact, die.)
3. They are without laws, agriculture, government, traditions, shipbuilding (and therefore have no foreign commerce), belief in the gods, and do not follow the rules of hospitality (for example, Polyphemus asks Odysseus questions without feeding him first—in fact, without feeding him at all).
4. Odysseus deceives Polyphemus about his name, lies about the whereabouts of his ship by claiming they were shipwrecked, and gets him drunk so he can put out his eye.
5. Answers will vary. Students may find that the blinding of Polyphemus or the eating of the companions sticks in their minds.
6. Instead of being third-person narration by the speaker/poet/performer/Homer, it becomes first-person narration by Odysseus.

## Strategy 12: Cross-Cultural Parallels—Fin MacCumhail, page 49
1. Students should note the following: The giant lives in a cave and keeps flocks. There is a fire in the cave. The giant does not treat the guests politely or feed them, but plans his own meal. The giant threatens to kill the guest. While the giant is asleep, the guest—using a heated stick found in the cave—puts out the giant's one eye. The giant awakes and blocks the only exit to the cave. The guest uses a member of the flock to escape from the cave.

## Writer's Forum: Comparison and Contrast, page 50
1. Students' essays should include the similarities they noted on Strategy 12 and the following contrasts: dog vs. men for companions; eating salmon vs. eating guests; open door vs. stone; goats vs. sheep; uncivilized behavior vs. uncivilized behavior with open hostility to the gods; knowledge from magic thumb vs. ingenuity.

## Book 10, pages 51–52
Answers will vary. Allow for individual opinion.
1. Aeolus believes that the gods have cursed Odysseus.
2. Dawn follows dusk, and the bay has high walls—this may be a description of a northern land (Land of the Midnight Sun) with fjords.
3. Students should note the following similarities: giants, cannibals, uncivilized, throw huge things at the boats. Differences: Cyclops did not appear to have females, families, or rulers; Cyclops did not unite to take action.
4. It is a poem of 4 stanzas of iambic tetrameter, each with the following rhyme scheme: ABABCCBC.
5. By his immunity to the drug and Hermes' prophecy that he would come.
6. The men who were in the group with Eurylochus are transformed into swine; Hermes transforms himself into a young man; the pigs are transformed back into men.
7. The other men prepared to follow Odysseus, but Eurylochus resisted, recalling to the group that Odysseus' poor judgment led to the death of the men at Polyphemus' hands.
8. Odysseus has revealed that they must travel to the Land of the Dead.

## Book 11, pages 53–54
Answers will vary. Allow for individual opinion.
1. Odysseus promises to bury Elpenor; Tiresias "promises" Odysseus that he will return home, kill the suitors, and die at sea at a good old age; and Alcinous promises Odysseus more gifts.
2. He must deny himself, restrain his shipmates, and avoid Helios' cattle.

3. He first says that Penelope cannot be a risk to Odysseus, but then he warns Odysseus to return to Ithaca secretly because wives are no longer faithful.
4. Answers will vary. Students may feel that the death of Iphigenia because of Agamemnon's rash promise began the chain of events. They may feel that whatever Agamemnon had done, Clytemnestra shouldn't have killed him.
5. Alcinous and his people are fascinated by Odysseus' artful telling and wish to hear more.
6. Answers will vary. Students should support their choice with reasons.
7. Students should note Achilles' comment comparing death and life and Anticleia's explanation of the differences between life and death.
8. Odysseus, Elpenor, Anticleia, and Agamemnon mention Telemachus. Among the shades who speak, Agamemnon mentions his own son (Orestes), Achilles mentions Neoptolemus. In his description of other shades, Odysseus mentions Tyro, wife of Aeolus' son, and her sons Pelias, Neleus, Aison, Pheres, and Amythaon; Antiope and her sons Amphion and Zethos; Alcmene and her son Heracles; Epicaste and her son Oedipus; Chloris and her sons Nestor, Chromios, and Periclymenos; Leda and her sons Castor and Polydeuces; Iphimedeia and her sons Otos and Ephialtes; Leto and her sons (who are not named). In addition, Agamemnon is referred to as "son of Atreus," Ajax is called "son of Telamon," and Odysseus is referred to as "son of Laertes." This seems to be the most important relationship, from the number of mentions. Students' other conclusions will vary.

## Strategy 13: Plot Elements, page 55

1. Students' answers may resemble the following (notice that the order of events is rearranged from Propp's list):
   - I. Odysseus leaves for the Trojan War.
   - VIIIa. Telemachus lacks his father and Penelope her husband.
   - XII. Athena speaks with Telemachus and tacitly agrees to become his helper.
   - IX. Athena dispatches Telemachus to find news of his father.
   - X. Telemachus agrees.
   - II. At the council, Telemachus is refused help.
   - III. Telemachus prepares to depart anyway.
   - XI. Telemachus leaves home.
   - IV./V. Antinous finds out about Telemachus from Noemon.
   - VI. Antinous plans to waylay and murder Telemachus.
2. Students' answers may resemble the following (notice that the order of events is rearranged from Propp's list):
   - XXIV. The suitors present unfounded claims to Odysseus' property and wife.
   - XXIII. Odysseus, unrecognized, arrives home.
   - XXV. The task of stringing the bow is proposed to Odysseus.
   - XXVI. Odysseus completes the task.
   - XXVIII. The suitors are exposed for what they are.
   - XXX. The suitors are punished by death.
   - XXIX. Athena gives Odysseus a new appearance.
   - XXVII. Penelope recognizes Odysseus.
   - XXXI. Odysseus and Penelope resume their marriage, and Odysseus resumes the kingship of Ithaca.

## Book 12, pages 56–57

Answers will vary. Allow for individual opinion.
1. The Sirens, Drifters, Scylla and Charybdis, and Helios' cattle; whether or not to listen to the Sirens' song, and what to tell his shipmates.
2. On the first page (all translations).
3. Answers may vary a little depending on the translation. Tiresias mentions that Helios sees and knows everything; says that if they stick to the sea, they will all reach Ithaca; warns that if they kill any cattle, the ship and crew will be destroyed and Odysseus will be the sole survivor, unable to return home for many years, but finally voyaging home on the ship of strangers to find his house full of rude suitors courting Penelope. Circe mentions the size of the flocks, their immortality, and that they do not calve; the shepherds who tend them, Helios' daughters; and ends with a warning almost verbatim of Tiresias' (in the Greek): that if they kill any cattle, the ship and crew will be destroyed and Odysseus will be the sole survivor and will not return home for many years.

4. Answers will vary. The Sirens claim to have knowledge of all the events of the Trojan War as well as of the future. You might wish to read Bernard Knox's comment on this to the class to encourage discussion: "Odysseus is a veteran of a ten-year war; he is on his way back to a society in which a new generation has grown up in peace. There will be no one to understand him if he talks about the war—it is significant that once home and recognized, he does not mention it to Telemachus or Penelope. Only those who shared its excitement and horrors with him can talk about it.... And that is the strength of the Sirens appeal.... But of course the Sirens' song is an invitation to live in the past, and that is a kind of death." Introduction to Fagles's translation, page 34.

5. The warning about Scylla and Charybdis. He says it is because it would not have benefited them—they would only have been terrified and abandoned their rowing (the implication being that they would then all have died). Answers may vary, but students will likely feel that he was justified in withholding information to save their lives.

6. Answers will vary. The basic idea is that, like a fisherman, Scylla reaches down from above, into the water, and pulls out her prey, which is then at her mercy.

7. Answers will vary. The points of comparison are as follows: In both, the leader withdraws to pray in solitude; in his absence, a trusted colleague is involved in a rebellion in which the people commit acts that have been prohibited, angering the god(s); the leader returns, and becoming aware of the prohibited celebration realizes that the people have lost the great god's favor. Also, in both, the sacrilege involves cattle.

8. Answers will vary. Answers may resemble the following: Driven back north between Scylla and Charybdis, but this time on Charybdis' side, Odysseus' raft got sucked into the whirlpool, and he leapt from it to grab onto the fig tree that overhangs Charybdis. There he hung until the whirlpool spit his raft up again, at which time he let go and fell onto his raft, and paddled with his hands to get past Scylla.

## Strategy 14: Theme, page 58

1. Answers will vary. Students may mention themes related to the following topics: order/disorder; hospitality; identity; desire for home; the meaning of true love/marriage; manhood/maturity; storytelling/poetry/art; returning from war; destiny/the meaning of life/people's relationship to the gods.

## Test 3: Books 9–12, page 59

1. Answers will vary. Students may think that the change adds interest and vividness to the account. They may say that hearing Odysseus tell both of his successes and his failures gives a unique insight into his character that wouldn't be there if the adventures were told in the third person.

2. Students should be aware of the marked difference in Odysseus' response to Anticleia from his response to the other dead, and also to the other deaths Odysseus has witnessed, and they may later see it as a portent of his tenderness toward Argos, Penelope, and Laertes. Although in many cases Odysseus is confrontational, with Ajax he tries, unsuccessfully, to make peace.

3. Answers will vary. Students may say that Odysseus uses cunning, intelligence, guile, liquor, primitive technology (if they see the tree trunk as a "tool"), organization, and leadership (in having his companions aid him). Answers to the comparison and contrast will vary depending on the stories the students choose, but most giant stories (from "Jack and the Beanstalk" to "Jack the Giant Killer") portray giants as having only brute strength and not much intelligence, and as being easily beaten by cunning and guile.

4. Aeolus—bag of winds: the remaining free wind brings him almost to Ithaca. Polyphemus—herds: provides food. Circe—advice, food, sacrificial animals: animals allow Odysseus to speak to Tiresias, Anticleia, etc.; the food keeps them alive on Thrinikia (Helios' island); advice allows Odysseus to evade the traps of the Sirens and Charybdis, and minimize the damage caused by Scylla. Tiresias— warnings, prophecies, advice: will allow Odysseus to fulfill his atonement to Poseidon.

5. Possible responses: The Sirens' recognition bolsters their claim to know everything, and makes them more enticing. Circe's recognition shows her divinity (even though she gets information from Hermes).

6. Students may speak to some of the following contrasts in their essay: Odysseus as host/stranger, master/beggar, king/storyteller. They may also write about order/disorder; peace/war; community/disunity.

7. In each, the crew arrives on an island with a herdsman (Polyphemus, Helios). In each, they take the herdsman's cattle. In each, the result is that missiles are hurled at their ship (a mountain top, a lightning bolt).

8. Answers will vary. Students' answers should account for the predictions of Circe and Tiresias, the prayer of Polyphemus, the decision of Zeus in response to Athena's plea for Odysseus, and the opening of the story.

## Book 13, pages 60–61

Answers will vary. Allow for individual opinion.
1. With the first line of Book 13, the poet/performer resumes narration.
2. They both long for their homecoming as the day wears on toward sunset.
3. Odysseus speaks of Penelope when Calypso dares him to compare them and find her wanting, when he speaks to Anticleia, and here, in Book 13. Students may mention the infrequency of references to Penelope, the depth of feeling he expresses when he speaks of her to Calypso, the emphasis on her fulfilling her duty rather than on how she herself is doing in his question to Anticleia, and/or the fact that here he mentions her first.
4. Answers will vary. Possible response: Considering that Zeus is the protector of strangers and the one who insists on hospitality to them and the Phaeacians are shining examples of that, it seems ironic that he agrees to the punishment that will lead them to behave in an inhospitable way.
5. He does not recognize Athena and does not trust anyone on Ithaca—perhaps he bears Agamemnon's warning in mind; perhaps he thinks that if he claims to be a murderer, others will be wary of him.
6. Odysseus tries to deceive Athena, Athena deceives Odysseus, Athena hides Odysseus in a mist, and Athena changes Odysseus' appearance to that of an old man.
7. Answers will vary. Pictures should match Homer's descriptions and convey Athena's power of disguise.

## Writer's Forum: Description, page 62

1. Students' descriptions should be based on the text. They should discuss the differences in the categories they use, features they describe, and organization of their two descriptions.

## Book 14, pages 63–64

Answers will vary. Allow for individual opinion.
1. It is possible that Odysseus is both preparing Eumaeus for a role he will have to take in helping Odysseus re-establish his rule and testing him to see if he is trustworthy.
2. Overall students should see the contrast between the true story (as far as we can judge) that Odysseus tells Alcinous and the made-up story that he tells Eumaeus. In both stories he gets married, goes to Troy, has adventures at sea, and is in a ship that is hit by a lightning bolt by Zeus. Just about everything else is different.
3. Eumaeus knows that the suitors are lying in wait to kill Telemachus on his way home.
4. Students may think that Odysseus would observe the host/guest relationship and exchange gifts with a host and that he would make up a scheme to trick a young soldier into giving up his cloak. They may also think that he rejoices in adventure. They may think that his claim to have no interest in farming, homelife, or children is false. They may also question whether he loves killing for its own sake.
5. Eumaeus has previously been tricked by someone claiming to have news of Odysseus, and he has seen how travelers take advantage of those who long for news of lost relatives.
6. If it turned out that the beggar was lying, the compact would call on Eumaeus to do something that would violate the host/guest relationship, and put him out of favor with Zeus.
7. Students may use words like *loyal, dutiful, protective, kind, patient, intelligent, trustworthy, savvy.*
8. Students may find nothing comparable besides the fact that they keep herds and guard them zealously. They may contrast Polyphemus' lone status, with Eumaeus' role, which is in the context of his duty to his master and his master's household.
9. He's trying to get Eumaeus to lend him a cloak.
10. Answers will vary depending on the translation, but Odysseus eventually calls Eumaeus by name, and Eumaeus (in all the translations but Rouse) calls the beggar "friend" in responding to the suggestion that they make a compact. It shows their growing camaraderie, despite the fact the Eumaeus does not believe the beggar's comments about Odysseus.

## Book 15, pages 65–66

Answers will vary. Allow for individual opinion.
1. Evidence in the text shows that the statement is not true of Penelope. Students may conjecture that Athena is telling lies to motivate Telemachus to leave quickly. Since Telemachus is not totally at ease with his mother (see Book 1), this may make it easier for him to believe Athena.

2. Answers will vary. Students may say that there are causes and beliefs that must be embraced wholeheartedly and without reservation in order to have any meaning or that when the extremes are in the realm of morality, taking the middle road is not appropriate. They may see room for the "middle" view in areas where the extremes can be conceived of as too much on the one hand and too little on the other: clothes, entertainment, food, etc.

3. Menelaus is most concerned with his guest's wishes, while Nestor is determined (by his son's account) to fulfill the demands of hospitality.

4. Answers will vary. Students may surmise that he will give an important prophecy or interpret an omen at a crucial moment.

5. Odysseus suggests that he will leave and go to town in order to see if Eumaeus will continue his hospitality.

6. Answers will vary. Commentators say that the first comment is ironic: Theoclymenus has asked which prince he can visit; since he cannot be a guest in Telemachus' house, the next choice would normally be the next greatest prince, although in this case, that would be inappropriate. Students may not see this.

7. In this book, Homer alternates between telling what is happening to Telemachus and what is happening to Odysseus. Students may see later or may conjecture now that it is a bridge to the following book where their separate stories join.

8. Answers will vary. Students may wonder if Odysseus will lie to Telemachus, too. They may comment on the fact that it seems that the meeting has been orchestrated to occur away from Odysseus' house at the home of the swineherd.

## Book 16, pages 67–68
Answers will vary. Allow for individual opinion.

1. Students may use words like *loving, loyal, tender, fatherly, sensitive, generous.*

2. He feels that because of his age and lack of training (and the lack of honor with which he is treated) that he is incapable of providing the protection the visitor deserves/requires.

3. Answers will vary. Possible responses: He is just playing out the part of the beggar, asking the question that any man without knowledge of the situation would ask. He is testing Telemachus to see what kind of man his son is. It is a way of finding out if Penelope has been faithful.

4. Suitors: 52 from Doulichion, 24 from Same, 20 from Zacyhnthos, and 12 from Ithaca, for a total of 108 suitors. In addition, there are 6 armorers, 2 servers, the crier and the harper (the last two will turn out to be loyal to Odysseus), or 10. The total is 118.

5. Students should mention that Odysseus and Telemachus will come to the house separately, Odysseus in his beggar's guise. Telemachus, at a sign, is to remove all weapons from the hall, save the ones that he and his father will use, giving an excuse that Odysseus has provided. Then they must learn which of the maids and male servants are corrupt and which are loyal. The plan ends there.

6. They make new plans to kill him because they are afraid he will go to the Counsel and reveal their plot, causing them to be exiled.

7. Antinous' father was saved by Odysseus, and Odysseus used to play with Eurymachus on his knee when Eurymachus was a child.

## Test 4: Books 13–16, page 69

1. Students may note that while Odysseus has other things to focus on (staying alive, adventures, the war, etc.), Penelope has little to do besides think of Odysseus. They may also note that both are "under siege," so to speak, and both manifest endurance, loyalty, intelligence, love, and cleverness in dealing with their respective situations.

2. Weaving (and unweaving) is the way that Penelope avoids the suitors for quite some time; Athena is the goddess of weaving, and Odysseus bids Athena to weave a plan for him. Weaving can also be used figuratively of storytelling, at which Odysseus is a master—so it might be said that they are all weavers.

3. Students should show recognition that it is incomplete at best—there is no strategy that deals with the odds of 118 to 2, and no reflection on where is the best location and how to begin.

4. Answers will vary. Students may mention the moment when Telemachus and Odysseus are reunited.

5. Possible response: Yes, because it is far more important to take care of the suitors and secure his house and Telemachus' life than to indulge his desire to see Penelope, which can wait 1 or 2 more days after an absence of 20 years.

6. Odysseus needs to be reunited with Laertes and Penelope. The suitors must die. Odysseus must propitiate Poseidon as Tiresias instructed him.

## Book 17, pages 70–71

Answers will vary. Allow for individual opinion.

1. Whatever incident students discuss, they should see that the 2 men carefully avoid direct interaction. The closest thing to direct speech is Odysseus' prayer after he receives Telemachus' gift of food from Eumaeus.
2. Answers will vary. Some students may see that if Theoclymenos, who doesn't know that Odysseus is in disguise, talks too much in public and people believe him, the beggar—the only stranger on the island that we have heard of—may come under suspicion and Athena's plan may be spoiled.
3. It seems like Medon is in league with the suitors, though the fact that he reported the plot to kill Telemachus to Penelope in Book 4 belies that.
4. Possible responses: patience, self-control, will-power, far-sightedness.
5. Students are likely to be moved by the dog's loyalty.
6. Answers will vary. Some students may feel that Athena is trying to make sure that Odysseus has experiences that will rouse his fighting spirit.
7. Students may first of all point out that, obviously, Odysseus is not going to tell the truth in this situation; second, that he tells a story that should gain him some respect: he has seen better times, and what has happened to him could happen to Antinous; third, that Odysseus seems to love to tell stories, so he'll take any opportunity.
8. Possible response: He may have gained increased acceptance of the death of the suitors, as opposed to lesser punishment.
9. Possible responses: That he is thoughtful, far-sighted, intelligent, clever.
10. Answers will vary.

## Strategy 15: Irony, page 72

1. Answers will vary. There are many, many examples of irony in the story. For example, it is ironic that Eumaeus' nurse, having herself been kidnapped and sold into slavery by pirates, is willing to do the same thing to Eumaeus on the chance that she will get home. It is ironic that Eumaeus, who was stolen from his parents and bought as a slave by Laertes, and so has real cause for resentment, should be the most loyal of Odysseus' servants and miss him more than he misses his own family.

## Book 18, pages 73–74

Answers will vary. Allow for individual opinion.

1. It seems to be a reference to his subservient nature.
2. He is trying to warn him so that Amphinomus can avoid the fate established for the suitors by Athena.
3. Answers will vary. Students may think that it was noble of Odysseus to anticipate that he might not return and release Penelope to marry again when she had brought up their son to adulthood.
4. Possible response: To test them.
5. Students may feel that, given his generosity and thoughtfulness, he should be spared.
6. Answers will vary. Drawings should reflect the text.

## Book 19, pages 75–76

Answers will vary. Allow for individual opinion.

1. In Book 16, Odysseus nods, Telemachus removes the weapons, making 1 or 2 excuses to the suitors, while leaving behind weapons for himself and Odysseus. In Book 19, the signal is given in speech, Odysseus and Telemachus remove the weapons together, the excuse is made to Eurycleia, although Odysseus has again referred to making the excuse to the suitors, Eurycleia is instructed to lock up the women (which seems to be an important part of the plan, although Odysseus has not mentioned it), and father and son both forget to provide themselves with weapons.
2. Answers will vary. Students may note that he hasn't seen his wife in 20 years and it is natural that he would look at her and remark on her beauty. They may think that he uses the ploy of saying that his history is too sad to tell in order to gain sympathy.

3. Answers will vary. Since he so closely describes possessions that belong to Odysseus, this may lead her to trust him. She may sense in some way that isn't conscious that he is Odysseus, or at least he might seem similar enough that she trusts him without exactly knowing why.

4. On several occasions, Homer praises Odysseus' artfulness in storytelling, which is perhaps a way of commenting on his own art.

5. Answers will vary. His description of Odysseus' clothing and brooch are accurate, but the setting in which he says he saw them is not true. Some of the details about his trip are true, after the introductory phrase in which he tells Penelope that he will say something true (the translations vary), and then says that Odysseus is alive and returning. The section following this is a mixture of truth (e.g., killing Helios' cattle) and falsehood (e.g., that the information comes from King Phidon).

6. Possible responses: Penelope cannot account rationally for her feelings about the beggar; she seems to be about to refer to the beggar as Odysseus when she asks Eurycleia to wash his feet; Eurycleia notices the similarity in body, voice, and limbs between the beggar and Odysseus.

7. Answers will vary. Students may think that it's for suspense, to keep the audience wondering what the recognition means; to answer the questions the audience would naturally have; or because there is little distinction between what is background and what is foreground in epic (see "Odysseus' Scar," by Erich Auerbach in his book *Mimesis*).

8. His life and the success of his plan for revenge depend on her silence.

9. He already knows, having had an opportunity to observe them himself.

10. Answers will vary. Some critics think that the contest of the bow is another ploy and that Penelope, knowing that no one but Odysseus can string the bow and do the feat, will be safe from the suitors. Others feel that her mention of Odysseus' explicit direction that she marry again means that she does intend to do as he wishes, despite her own inclinations. Students may agree with one of these views, or voice a different opinion.

## Writer's Forum: Anecdote, page 77

1. Answers will vary. Students' anecdotes should fit with information from the *Odyssey* and with the general tenor of the epic, but may include made-up details. The anecdote form should be clear. If students write about the bow, have them compare their anecdotes with Homer's at the opening of Book 21.

## Book 20, pages 78–79

Answers will vary. Allow for individual opinion.
1. Possible response: his restlessness and inner discomfort.
2. Athena does not give Odysseus a plan. She just asks him to trust her and to go to sleep.
3. Answers will vary. Students may think that he is so concerned about Odysseus that he'll say anything as an excuse to ask for information or that he is playing a role in case the suitors are listening.
4. The suitors do not offer sacrifice.
5. Telemachus speaks to the suitors as master of the house, telling them how they may and may not behave in his hall, and he is confident enough to ignore Antinous.
6. Possible responses: to increase his wrath; to justify their deaths.
7. Possible response: Because, unbeknownst to them, some of what they say is true: (Fitzgerald) Telemachus would agree that he is a lucky host to have such a guest as the beggar (his father), although they say it sarcastically; (Rouse, Fagles, Lattimore) Telemachus would agree that he is an unlucky host—to have such guests as the suitors in his house.
8. Answers will vary. Students should support their opinions with evidence.

## Test 5: Books 17–20, page 80

1. He's been attacked by Eumaeus' dogs, Antinous with his footstool, Eurymachus with his footstool, Ktesippos with the cow foot, Irus in a boxing match, Melanthius and Melantho and the suitors with words. Answers will vary. They increase his anger, justify the death of the suitors, and lend irony to the homecoming (in what sense is he home?). Answers will vary. They are from men and women, not monsters and deities; they are from those who should be loyal, not from strangers; they take place within what should be the domain he rules, not out in the wide world in foreign lands.

2. He is living without his name, inheritance, ancestry, true form and figure, and wife.
3. He is the one who asks Demodocus for the song that ends up making him weep and leads to Alcinous urging that he reveal himself. He asks for a loyal old lady to wash him when she is the only one who can recognize him.
4. Answers will vary, partly depending on how students interpret what Penelope IS doing (setting an impossible contest that will free her from the suitors' intentions; giving in; following Odysseus' wishes, etc.).
5. Answers will vary. Students may find it inconceivable that anyone but Odysseus can string the bow, so they may predict that he will reveal himself and string his bow. They may also see the strategic possibilities of having a bow (as opposed to a sword or spear) when 2 are fighting against 108 or 118.
6. Answers will vary. Accept reasonable responses.
7. Answers will vary. Students may mention the lack of shared experience, growth in different directions, expectations.

## Book 21, pages 81–82
Answers will vary. Allow for individual opinion.
1. Students should notice expressions such as the following (these are from Fitzgerald's translation) "quills of groaning" (391), "the quiver spiked with coughing death" (392), "Antinous, destined to be the first of all to savor blood from a biting arrow at his throat" (394).
2. Answers will vary. Students' responses should be grounded in the text.
3. Possible response: It may be a response to the irony of Antinous' statements, "I can see him [Odysseus] even now" (Fitzgerald), or "There is not a man in all this company as good as Odysseus" (Rouse), or "that bow . . . our crucial test that makes or breaks us" (Fagles). He explains it as being a kind of embarrassed/relieved reaction to his mother's change of heart.
4. Because Odysseus signaled to him not to. Students may consider that if Telemachus had strung the bow straight off, the suitors' focus might have turned to wrath against him and they might have attacked him before Odysseus was in possession of the bow.
5. Students may take either side, but should support their stances with reasons.
6. I. They should return separately to avoid arousing suspicion. II. Eumaeus is to bring Odysseus the bow so that he is armed to fight the suitors (only a weapon of this sort—not hand-to-hand—can allow a few combatants to take on many). III. The women are to be out of the way for their physical safety, so the maids who have lovers among the suitors do not interfere, so the suitors cannot go there to hide among the women, and to preserve the women from the horror that will follow. IV. The outer gate is to be locked so that the suitors cannot escape their fate and so that no one else can come to their aid.
7. Students may point out the following in their answers: Antinous has clearly not tried the bow when he gives it to Leodes. There is no explicit reference or description in the text of Antinous trying the bow. It says at one point that no one was able to string it, but Antinous and Eurymachus held off and waited. Antinous' suggestion to leave the contest for the next day may be to get out of trying and failing in front of the others. It may seem unlikely that Homer would lose an opportunity to show Antinous at a disadvantage.
8. That they wait till the next day, make sacrifice to Apollo, and try again.
9. Answers will vary. Possible responses: He is trying to show his father that he is a son worthy of him. It is just a continuation of the change he showed in Book 20, when he declared himself master in his own home. He knows that it is time to get Penelope out of the way, and he uses this means to effect that.
10. Answers will vary, but students may (1) see the bow as his means of attaining lasting fame as musicians do through their music; (2) see his skill with the bow as comparable to a musician's skill with an instrument; and/or (3) see an implicit comparison between Odysseus and Homer, recalling earlier comparisons of Odysseus to a minstrel.
11. Most students will predict a fight in which all the suitors are killed.

## Strategy 16: Foreshadowing and Flashback, page 83
1. The sections of the text that are anecdotes are flashbacks, for example, the story of the scar. What is essential information will vary with the particular example chosen.
2. Students may refer to the appearance of birds, the sound of thunder, the maid's prayer, or Telemachus' sneeze. Students may observe that they are absolutely certain predictors—there is not an inaccurate or misunderstood omen in this story.

3. Students may mention the descriptions of the arrows with expressions such as the following: (these are from Fitzgerald's translation) "quills of groaning" (391); "the quiver spiked with coughing death" (392); the direct statement about Antinous' death in Book XXI: "Antinous, destined to be the first of all to savor blood from a biting arrow at his throat" (394) back to the first reference to the death of the suitors made by Athena (in the guise of Mentes) to Telemachus in Book I: "it will be time to ponder concerning these contenders in your house —how you should kill them . . ." (10); and other references to the death of the suitors and comparisons between Telemachus and Orestes.

## Book 22, pages 84–85

Answers will vary. Allow for individual opinion.

1. Answers will vary. Students may feel that Eurymachus is scapegoating Antinous (who can't respond because he's dead) and not taking responsibility for his own actions; or that he is telling the truth. Given that, they may find his proposal just or unjust. Even if they find it just, they may see that it is impossible for Odysseus to accept because the suitors' deaths have been decreed by the gods (students should remember that Odysseus himself tried to save Amphinomus, but could not, for this very reason).
2. The bow allows Odysseus to hold off a crowd of men with a single weapon. When the arrows run out, arms are needed.
3. Possible response: Medon's escape from death, wrapped in a bull's skin, is reminiscent of Odysseus' escape from Polyphemus, and bespeaks his creative intelligence. The harper and Odysseus are both tellers of many tales, masters of artful speech.
4. Answers will vary. Students may appreciate the vivid imagery and careful detail, or they may not care for it.
5. Answers will vary. Possible response: The written manuscript that was passed down to us draws on two different versions of the sung epic—one in which the identification of the disloyal maids by Odysseus played a part, and one in which Eurycleia simply identified them for him.
6. In both situations the contest begins with him as an onlooker. He is jeered by the contestants, but ends up, unexpectedly, besting them in the appointed sport.
7. Answers will vary. Students may think that he is finally relaxing and allowing himself to feel the emotions of coming home, and also allowing himself to experience his longing for Penelope.

## Book 23, pages 86–87

Answers will vary. Allow for individual opinion.

1. After the speech in which Eurycleia identifies Odysseus with the stranger, it seems as if Penelope might be beginning to believe her. Answers as to why will vary—maybe she has had the same thought herself—both Eurycleia and Philoitios remarked on the likeness between the stranger and Odysseus, so it would be natural for Penelope to notice it, although this is not stated.
2. She suggests that a god is responsible. Answers will vary.
3. Maybe she is afraid to have her hopes dashed again or afraid of being deceived.
4. Answers will vary. Students may mention patience, love, generosity, understanding, devotion.
5. The pretense of a wedding at Odysseus' home; Penelope's pretense that Odysseus' bed has been moved. Students may or may not mention Athena's enhancement of Odysseus' looks.
6. Answers will vary. Literary critics disagree about this, so it is likely that students will, also.

## Strategy 17: Character Traits, page 88

1. & 2. Answers will vary depending on students' interpretations of characters' actions. For example: Is part of what goes into Penelope's decision to have the contest of the bow confidence that no one but Odysseus can string it and make the shot? Is Odysseus' choice to visit the Cyclops irresponsible? Allow for reasonable interpretations.

## Book 24, pages 89–90

Answers will vary. Allow for individual opinion.

1. Amphimedon tells Agamemnon: that Penelope wished for the suitors' death (in the Lattimore, Rouse, and Fagles translations); how Zeus told Telemachus to move the arms to the storeroom and lock it, and Odysseus told Penelope to have the contest of the bow (these details differ from the tale Homer has told); how Telemachus insisted the beggar be given the bow (he doesn't mention that Penelope also insisted); how Odysseus was eventually joined in battle by a god (he doesn't mention Telemachus and the two herdsmen) until all the suitors were dead. Students may think that these changes are to gain sympathy or may result from combining different oral versions of the tale into one written version.

2. Answers will vary. Some students may think that it is cruel. Some may believe that it is a way of bringing Laertes to think about Odysseus so that his sudden appearance will not be too great a shock for the old man.

3. Answers will vary. Some may say that he is an inveterate storyteller. All the translators except Lattimore show by their English translations that the Greek names that Odysseus uses in this tale have meaning, and make the story almost allegorical. Students who read one of these translations may respond to that element of Odysseus' story.

4. Possible response: Those who are convinced by Eupithes are moved by pity for his tears and his words. Those who are convinced by Medon are moved to fear by his report of seeing a god. And Halitherses appeals to their moral sense.

5. Answers will vary. Students should support their answers with reasons.

## Writer's Forum: Compare and Contrast a Book and a Movie, page 91

Students should address the questions given for guidance. Facts and opinions should be clearly stated and opinions should be supported by evidence.

## Test 6: Books 21–24, page 92

1. These are the elements that Powell finds "strongly present":
   a. Calypso Ia, Ib, IIIb, IV, IVa, IVd, IVe, IVg, V, VI, X
   b. Polyphemus Ia, II, IV, IVa, IVb, IVc, IVd, IVe, IVf, IVg, IVh, V, VI, VII, VIIIa, IX, XI, XII, XIVb, XV
   c. Aeolus Ia, Ib, II, III, IV, IVe, IVf, IVg, IVh, V, VI, VII, VIIIa, XI, XIVb
   d. Circe Ia, II, III, IV, IVe, IVf, IVg, IVh, V, VI, VII, VIIIa, IX, X, XId, XII, XIII, XIVa, XV
   e. the Suitors IV, IVa, IVc, V, VI, VII, VIIIa, VIIIb, IX, X, XI, XId, XII, XIII

2. Students who look at the bulk of the story and count up the episodes are likely to classify it as adventure. Students who privilege the end are likely to call it a love story. Some students may refuse to choose and say it is both.

3. Answers will vary. Students should explain their choices.

4. Answers will vary. Students should show some depth in their engagement with the story or explain clearly why it did not engage them.